LEARNING LAW

The Mastery of Legal Logic

D1525374

LEARNING LAW

The Mastery of Legal Logic

SHELDON MARGULIES
KENNETH LASSON

CAROLINA
ACADEMIC
PRESS
700 KENT ST.
DURHAM, NC
27701

Carolina Academic Press
700 Kent Street at Duke University Road
Durham, North Carolina 27701

(919) 489-7486
FAX (919) 493-5668

CONTENTS

LEARNING LAW
The Mastery of Legal Logic

Overview of an Overview

For most students law school often seems like a tedious series of unrelated courses, each semester focusing on a new and distinct area of jurisprudence. The purpose of this book is to bring the whole curriculum into perspective by explaining the basic legal principles governing almost all lawsuits.

A case begins when someone is injured or about to be injured. In a civilized society the victim's primary means of self-defense is the law; it is the best way to keep potential transgressors from violating accepted principles of fair play. The law imposes upon us various duties that restrict behavior—often in rather specific ways. When we fail to conform to these restrictions without a good excuse, we are considered "in breach." Anyone injured as a result is entitled to relief, usually in the form of money (damages); a prohibition of similar injurious acts in the future; or an order directing the defendant to carry out a specific act.

Building Blocks of the Law

Legally enforceable duties derive from eight major areas of jurisprudence:

CONTRACTS   COMMON LAW
WARRANTIES   STATUTES
TORTS   CONSTITUTIONAL LAW
CRIMINAL LAW   EQUITY

Common law, statutes, equity, and constitutional law are foundations from which the laws governing contracts, torts, warranties, and criminal law are derived. Here are nutshell definitions of the areas mentioned:

Contracts—two or more parties agree to perform according to specific terms and conditions

Warranties—the guarantees included with a purchased product or service

Torts—personal injuries wrongfully caused by others

Equity—the application of fairness when the "black-letter" law is not otherwise on your side

Common Law—law developed independently by judges over a long period of time, where the legislature has not already passed a controlling statute

Statutes—laws enacted by state legislatures or by Congress

Constitutional Law—whatever the Constitution says, according to the Supreme Court

Criminal Law—a mixture of statutory, common, and constitutional law defining criminal activity.

Other branches of the law—property, estates and trusts, domestic relations, admiralty and so on—are in turn built upon those areas noted above. For example, property law combines the common law, statutes, equity, and constitutional law, as well as the law of contracts, warranties, and torts.

Building Blocks of the Law

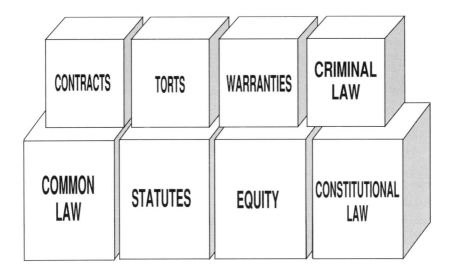

Each branch of the law carries with it various duties of performance. Failure to perform allows an injured party—once he determines which duty was breached—to win redress of his grievances. Unfortunately, only a small (but critical) portion of a student's time is spent working backward and figuring out, from the facts at hand, which branch of the law applies. The vast majority of law school training is concerned with learning the duties each branch of the law imposes on us, the procedures involved in bringing your case before the proper court within the proper time frame, and with presenting the most effective arguments.

From a lawyer's perspective, a typical case may be analyzed as follows:

A client has suffered some financial, physical, or emotional injury. The lawyer's job is to work backward by first determining what caused the damage, then sorting through each branch of the law to see whether the client's injury was caused by a breach of some legally defined duty owed him. If you as a lawyer can find both breach and causation, your client may now become a plaintiff in a "cause of action." Where breach of a duty amounts to a crime, the state becomes the plaintiff and can sue (prosecute) under a criminal indictment.

Whether the defendant owed your client a duty to perform is actually a two-part question: did the defendant owe a duty and, if so, did he owe that duty to your client? Sometimes *several* branches of the law impose a duty of performance on the defendant, allowing the plaintiff to sue under more than one cause of action. The second part—establishing a legal relationship between the defendant and your client—depends on the triggering event that brought the parties together. That event may have been a contract, a purchase of merchandise, an interest in property, proximity to a hazardous situation, an intentional physical or verbal attack, and so on. The triggering event determines the branch of law governing the case.

Issues in a Lawsuit

The first two questions, then, are (1) which branch of the law applies? and (2) does a legal relationship exist between the parties under that branch of the law? Suppose, for example, the plaintiff was injured by the defendant and now seeks to sue him.

Which branch of the law applies?

Contract law	Real property
Torts	Warranty
	Constitutional law

Was there a valid contract between the parties? Was one party of interest a third-party beneficiary? (**contract law**)

Was there a valid legal relationship? (**torts**)

Was there a valid purchase covered by a valid warranty? (**warranty**)

What interest in property created the relationship? Was that property valid? (**real property**)

Were the parties in a partnership, employer-employee, independent, contractor, principal-agent, landlord-tenant, or fiduciary relationip? (**common law**)

Had a corporation formed? If so, what was the legal relationship of the parties to the corporation? (**statutory law**)

One cannot sue without first finding some legal relationship imposing a duty of performance on the defendant. Moreover, when things go wrong, the responsible party may not be the one the plaintiff is suing, or there may be more responsible parties than the plaintiff thought. This happens in four common situations: when a property is sublet, when an agent acts on behalf of a principal, when an independent contractor is hired to do a specific job, and when there are partnerships and limited partnerships.

When a tenant subleases his property, he retains responsibility for the rent. When he *assigns* the lease, he turns over responsibility for the rent to the sublessee.

When an agent works for a principal, the principal is responsible for any commitments made by the agent, as long as the agent was acting within the scope of his responsibility. If either the agent or the person dealing with the agent reasonably thought the agent was working on behalf of a principal, the principal is responsible for the agent's commitments.

Like a principal, an employer is responsible for an employee as long as the employee was acting within the scope of his employment. An employer is not responsible for the acts of an independent contractor. Even though he is hired by the employer, the independent contractor controls his own work and therefore bears responsibility for any breaches.

Partners are fully responsible for each other as long as the breaching partner was acting on behalf of the partnership. A *limited* partner is only liable up to the amount of his investment, but he can lose his limited partnership status by acting as a general partner—usually defined as taking part in the control of the partnership.

If the plaintiff is claiming that the defendant was acting on behalf of a partnership, he must prove that a partnership existed and not— for example—a principal-agent relationship. If the plaintiff is claiming the defendant was acting on behalf of a corporation, he must prove that a corporation had formed and had not yet dissolved.

Was There A Duty?

Given a legal relationship between the parties, what duty was owed to the plaintiff by the defendant?

Was There A Breach?

If the defendant did owe the plaintiff a duty, did he breach (violate) it?

Was There An Excuse?

Breach is a term of art, defined as an *unexcused* failure to perform. Deciding when someone has failed to perform his legal duty is not always easy—but the harder question is whether the defendant may be excused *despite* his nonperformance.

The law is forgiving to defendants. It excuses their nonperformance in a variety of circumstances, sometimes simply because of who the defendant is. Likewise, the law may protect the defendant because of some inexcusable behavior by the *plaintiff*. And sometimes a court may rule that the law itself, not the defendant, was wrong (unconstitutional, for example).

Was There A Provable Injury?

Even if the plaintiff can prove the defendant in breach of a duty owed to him, that does not always mean he will collect. He still must show that he was in fact injured, and that the defendant's breach is what actually caused the injury. Proving injury is a relatively straight-forward process; proving "causation" can be a lot more slippery because not only does the plaintiff have to prove that the defendant's breach caused his injury, but also that the injury was reasonably foreseeable.

In summary, it's as simple as this: If an injured client wants to sue a defendant, the plaintiff's lawyer will need to prove duty, breach, causation, and injury. Answer these questions and you have a case:

• Which branch of the law says the defendant owed your client a duty?

• Was a legal relationship established between the defendant and your client?

• As a result of that legal relationship, what duty did the defendant owe your client?

• Did the defendant fail to perform that legal duty?

• Was the defendant's failure to perform the legal duty nevertheless excusable?

• Did the defendant's breach actually and foreseeably cause your client's injury?

• What exactly was your client's injury?

• Finally, what do you want the court to do about it—that is, what remedy would satisfy your client?

Battle Lines

At this point you should already see where the legal battles will take place. The defendant will offer one or more of the following arguments:

• I didn't owe your client a duty because we had no legally enforce-able relationship.

• I didn't breach because the plaintiff is mistaken about what happened; I did perform.

• I didn't breach because the plaintiff is mistaken about the duty imposed on me by the law; I did perform what the law demanded.

• Yes, I failed to perform, but I am not in breach because I had a good excuse for not performing.

• Yes, I failed to perform without an excuse (breach), but you can't sue me, either because I can't be sued, or because you have no right to sue me.

• I didn't breach because the law that says I breached is either unconstitutional or wrong by today's standards.

• Yes, I breached, but my breach is not what caused your injury.

• Yes, I breached, but your injury was not foreseeable.

• Yes, I breached, but you never suffered any injury from my breach.

With this broad overview in mind, we can now examine contracts, warranties, and tort law for a closer look at how the battle lines are drawn—and at the way common law, statutes, equity, and Constitutional law interact in various situations.

Did the Defendant Owe the Plaintiff a Duty?

Standing

Was there a legal relationship between the plaintiff and the defendant? In order to prevail in a lawsuit a plaintiff must be able to prove that a defendant owed him a duty. Without such proof a plaintiff is said to lack "standing"—the legal version of "It's none of your business." To have standing to sue, the plaintiff must also have suffered (or be about to suffer) an actual injury, called injury-in-fact.

Under contract law, the plaintiff has standing if there is "privity of contract." About the only time standing is bestowed on someone *not* a party to a contract is when the plaintiff is a third party that the contract has named as the beneficiary of the agreement. A life insurance policy is an example of a third-party beneficiary contract. The insurer and the insured are the primary parties to the contract; the third-party beneficiary is the beneficiary named on the policy. Even in third-party beneficiary contracts, the plaintiff gains standing only when (having learned that he is the intended beneficiary) he either notifies the parties that he agrees to that status or relies on it to his detriment.

Under tort law, a plaintiff has standing if he is "foreseeable"—that is, if the defendant could reasonably have foreseen that he would injure the plaintiff. For example, an automobile driver negligently causes an auto accident. A tow truck on its way to the scene hits a pedestrian. The pedestrian cannot sue the automobile driver for his injuries, because he was not a foreseeable victim. (In suits under product liability, standing is often extended to anyone who might reasonably use a product.)

Contracts

If two parties make a legally enforceable contract, they owe each other a duty to perform according to its terms. Whether a contract is legally enforceable depends on its subject matter: if the contract is for goods (things that can be moved), it is governed by a statute called the Uniform Commercial Code (UCC); everything else (real estate, employment, and contracts for services) is governed by the common law.

The UCC and the common law generally agree on the ingredients of an enforceable contract. There must be (1) a clear offer containing unambiguous essential terms; (2) a clear acceptance of that offer; (3) consideration; (4) freely consenting parties; and (5) a legal purpose to the contract. Under some circumstances, the contract must be in writing and signed by the party being sued. Offer, acceptance, consideration, consent, legality, and a signed writing are called "elements" of an enforceable contract.

Offer

An offer is a promise to stand behind a proposal. As soon as the offer is accepted by the "offeree," both parties are bound—assuming that they both *intended* to make an agreement. Thus, offers made in jest or in anger are not valid if the offeror did not intend to be bound. Who decides what the offeror intended? The law looks to what a "reasonable man" would think about the agreement. If the offeror actually believed he was joking when he made the offer—but a reasonable observer thought he was serious—then the offeror will be bound by his proposal. (Not an offer: "I'm so fed up with my car, I'd sell it for a thousand dollars!" Possibly an offer: "Please buy my husband's boat before it destroys our marriage—he'd sell it for a thousand dollars!" An offer: "If you sign a contract today, I'll sell you my house for $50,000.")

A reward is a valid offer, but advertisements are not. Interpreting common law, the courts have said that an advertiser is not willing to be bound by his ad in case he runs out of the item being advertised. Similarly, offers made to more than one person are not true offers so long as it is reasonably clear to each offeree that the offer was also being made to others and not to him alone.

Likewise, invitations to make an offer, inquiries about a potential sale, and statements of willingness to be bound sometime in the future are not offers—because they do not represent a clear willingness by the offeror to be bound immediately if the offeree chooses to accept. "I am interested in buying your car next month for $3000" is not a valid offer." Nor is, "I'm calling to inquire if you would be willing to sell your house for $100,000."

The terms of an offer must be clear enough so that if the offeree does accept, the two parties (and the court) will know what was agreed upon. Thus, "essential terms" must be included in an offer. Both the UCC and the common law agree that one of those terms must be the quantity of the item bargained for. Under the common law the price must also be included; the UCC is willing to let the parties agree later on the price (and if they can't agree, the court will impose a reasonable price based on fair market value). Neither the common law nor the UCC generally requires that quality or delivery terms be included, although those provisions can help confirm the seriousness with which the offer was made. Unless an offer has satisfied these minimal legal requirements—willingness to be bound immediately and unambiguous essential terms—any "acceptance" is meaningless and no duty will be imposed on either party. "I accept your offer to sell Jumbo Brand Hot Dogs for thirty-five cents each" is not a valid acceptance, because the quantity is omitted. Nor is this: "Next Monday I will accept your offer to sell a hundred Jumbo Brand Hot Dogs for thirty-five cents each. Please deliver by Friday." The acceptance here does not reflect a willingness to be bound immediately.

What if the offer was valid, but was withdrawn before acceptance? Where there is no offer to accept, there can be no contract. When can offers be withdrawn? Under the common law, offers can almost always be withdrawn (revoked) prior to acceptance—even if the offeror *promised* to keep the offer open. The only way an offeror can be forced to keep the offer open is if he has been paid to do so; this is called an option contract. The UCC is less strict: an offer can be made irrevocable ("firm"), but only if it is made by a merchant in a signed writing with assurances that the offer will be held open. Even this kind of offer is revocable if the item is sold and the offeree learns of the sale before accepting. (If the offeree did not know of the sale when he accepted, he may have a cause of action against the offeror for having sold the item counter to his firm offer.)

Although the common law almost always allows an offeror to withdraw his offer before acceptance, it *insists* on such a revocation if the offeror expects to avoid being legally bound. Example: an item is offered for sale to more than one person, and then sold; unless the offeror notifies everyone of the sale, he will be bound by additional sales contracts if other offerees accept before learning of the sale.

An offer is also irrevocable if, before it has been withdrawn, the offeree begins *performing* an acceptance. Example: An offeror says he will pay $5 to have his car washed. The offeree can accept by beginning to wash the car without formally saying "I accept." (The offer can be revoked even after the offeree has paid for the soap and sponges, so long as he has not yet begun to wash the car.)

An offer is automatically withdrawn by destruction of the thing being offered, by supervening illegality of the contract, or by the death or mental disability of the offeror. Thus, destruction of a building by fire automatically revokes an offer to sell it. Likewise, a new statute outlawing gambling revokes an offer to sell gambling equipment. Sudden confinement of the offeror to a mental institution serves to revoke an offer he's made previously.

An offer cannot be accepted after it has been rejected or a counteroffer made. Whether an offer was in fact rejected depends on an objective interpretation of what the offeree said. If the offer is said to be "firm," it cannot be terminated by either rejection or counteroffer.

Acceptance

To be valid under the common law, an acceptance must satisfy four requirements:

1) *Only the offeree can accept.* That makes sense. The offeror has full control over his offer and he can direct it to whomever he wants. If the offer is made to a group of people, anyone in that group may accept. Thus Bill's brother cannot accept an offer made to Bill, but he can accept one made to Bill's family.

2) *The offeree must know of the offer at the time he accepts.* For example, a person who apprehends a criminal cannot collect the reward if he turns him in without realizing a reward was being offered.

3) *The offeree can only accept what is offered.* That is, he cannot vary the terms of the offer. This is known as "the mirror image rule" and under the common law is strictly adhered to. The offeree cannot argue that he changed only a non-essential term—since the offeror has full control over his offer, everything in it is deemed essential to him. The only new terms permitted in the acceptance are those which would automatically be included in the offer. For example, if the offeror were selling a service contract, the law automatically infers that the job would be done in a workmanlike manner.

Just as the offeror is in full control of his offer, he can also control the manner of acceptance. Thus, if he wants the offeree to accept by certified check, acceptance can *only* be made by certified check.

Acceptance under the UCC is considerably different than under the common law. For example, if either the offeror or the offeree is not a merchant, the offeree is held to have accepted the original offer even if his acceptance varies the terms of the offer! The variations are construed merely as *proposals* for changing the contract which the offeror is free to accept or reject. Unless the offeree stipulates that he is accepting only if his new terms are incorporated into the contract, he will be held to the original offer. Valid: "I accept your offer but I would like to change the delivery time to Saturday, December 7th." (The offeror, of course, can object to the proposed change—see below.) Not valid: "I accept your offer on the condition that delivery take place on Saturday, December 7th." (This is a counter-offer which the offeror must now accept in order to make a valid contract.)

If the offeror and offeree are both merchants, terms in the acceptance which vary the offer are not discarded. They will be incorporated into the contract to the extent that the variations merely add to the agreement without materially changing it—unless the offeror objects to the additional terms within a reasonable time. Thus, between merchants, "I accept your offer but I would like to change the delivery time to Saturday, December 7th" is a valid acceptance (incorporating the new delivery date) unless the offeror objects to the proposed change within a reasonable time.

4) *The offeree must communicate his acceptance to the offeror.* This places the burden on the offeree to notify the offeror. But even if he doesn't, the offeror is bound to the agreement if he *should* have known of the offeree's acceptance. For example, if Yuppy offers Slapdash $500 to paint his house and Slapdash does the job, Yuppy will owe Slapdash $500 because he *should* have known that his house was being painted.

If Slapdash responds to Yuppy's offer by mailing him a letter promising to paint his house in one week, acceptance occurred the moment Slapdash put the letter in the mailbox—the so-called "mailbox rule." On the other hand, the offeror's mailed revocation or the offeree's mailed rejection of an offer become effective only on receipt of the letter.

Consideration

Consideration is what each party gives up in order to get what he wants. In a sale, the trade is goods for money, but almost anything of value will suffice for consideration. Even a promise to do something or refrain from doing something is valid consideration. Thus, one party can give up his legal right to sue another party in return for monetary consideration. For example, for an agreed-upon sum one can give up the right to contest a will after the testator dies.

If the offeree gives no consideration, the offer becomes merely a promise to give a gift. The promisee may agree to "accept" the promise, but there is no contract. Contracts are enforceable; promises to give gifts are not. If the promisor changes his mind, there is nothing the promisee can do because the promise of a gift is merely a gratuitous gesture, not the result of a bargain. Because the promisee never gave up anything, he never lost anything when the promise was withdrawn. Not enforceable for lack of consideration: "I promise to give you $100 next week." Enforceable: "I promise to give you $100 next week for that 1959 Billy Pierce baseball card."

Consideration may also be viewed as something given up in response to a conditional offer. The offeror says, "I promise to do this if you do that." If you do what the offeror asks, you will have given consideration, because that's what he bargained for. Thus, "I promise to give you $20 if you mow my lawn" is enforceable because each side gives up something to secure the bargain.

Both the offeror and the offeree must give consideration. This simple idea places some very real restrictions on the kinds of things that will suffice for consideration. For example, if a painter has already promised to paint someone's house for $1000, he cannot raise his price; a new promise to paint the house for $1200 is not supported by any new consideration on his part. This concept of a "pre-existing duty" prevents an unscrupulous person from extracting more money once the other party is already committed.

On the other hand, the two parties can modify their contract simply by providing new consideration on either side. For example, the painter can promise to paint faster or use a different color in exchange for a higher fee. The UCC does away with the need for new consideration when modifying a contract, so long as each party exercises "good faith."

Consideration must be new, representing something given up by one party to secure the other party's performance. Suppose Slapdash decides after painting the house for $1000 that his fee was $200 too high; to relieve his conscience, he tells the homeowner that he will paint the garage for free. Hasn't there been consideration by both sides—the painter's promise to paint the garage and the homeowner's $200 overpayment? No, the $200 overpayment is not new; it is "past consideration." Thus, Slapdash can withdraw his promise to paint the garage without being in breach.

"Illusory" promises are also unenforceable. These are promises over which the offeror retains so much control that he is not really giving up anything. For example, if our painter offers "to paint the house on Wednesday for $1000, assuming I feel like painting that day," he can change his mind up to the last second without breaching this promise.

Thus, contracts based on a pre-existing duty, past consideration, and illusory promises are unenforceable for want of proper consideration.

Consent

In contracts, each party voluntarily consents to have a duty placed upon him. Under the law of torts, warranty, property, and estates and trusts, a duty is automatically imposed upon the parties by the state legislatures and the courts—without anyone's express consent.

Consent is a necessary element of an enforceable contract, and requires that (1) the person granting consent must have the authority to do so; (2) the consent must be given voluntarily; and (3) the consent must be based on a reasonable disclosure of the facts necessary to make an informed decision.

Authority

Not everyone has the authority or "capacity" to consent to a contractual obligation. A person must be reasonably able to judge what is in his best interests. This rule protects the young, the mentally disabled, the intoxicated, and anyone else the court decides to place under a guardianship.

The only subtlety about capacity is the difference between a *void* contract—one that was never legally binding—and a *voidable* contract, a valid agreement that can be voided by the legally disabled party. Minors, the mentally ill, and the intoxicated make voidable contracts. Those made by people under a guardianship are void.

A special rule was created to protect those selling necessaries (food, clothing, and shelter) to minors. The law gives the minor a choice: either he pays for what he's used or he returns it. The law is less sympathetic to those contracting with minors for something other than necessaries. Although the minor must return whatever goods are still in his possession, he can keep whatever he's used without having to pay for them.

A contract entered into by an intoxicated person is voidable, but only if he was so intoxicated that he couldn't form rational judgments when he signed the agreement—and the other party had good reason to know that. Even then, the intoxicated party will be bound by the contract if he doesn't quickly disaffirm it when he sobers up, returning any consideration he may have received.

Authority to be bound to a contract can be delegated to another person under a "principal-agent" relationship. A principal is bound to a contract signed by his agent so long as signing contracts was within the scope of the agent's authority. If the principal neither expressly granted authority to his agent to contract on his behalf, nor ratified the unauthorized contract, the law will nonetheless hold the principal accountable if either the agent or the third party reasonably thought the agent had proper authority. Thus, if a salesman had conducted business on the owner's behalf in the past, and the owner gave no indication to either the salesman or the customer of any change in the salesman's responsibilities, the owner will be held accountable for any business the salesman conducts on his behalf.

Voluntariness

Consent must be given voluntarily—not under duress, necessity, or undue influence. Duress is a direct threat against the person consenting. Necessity is a threat to something external to the person, like job security. Undue influence occurs when someone extracts a consent because he is loved or feared by the consenting party. Thus, if an employer hands his employee a new contract containing a burdensome clause and the employee signs under threat of being fired ("Take it or leave!"), the contract may not be enforceable. But if a prospective employee signs the same contract because he needs a job, a court might find that the threat of continued unemployment is insufficient duress to render the contract unenforceable.

Informed Consent

Fairness is the cornerstone of the law. What could be less fair than misleading someone into signing a contract by misstating an important fact? In such a case, the law will make the contract voidable, allowing the innocent party the choice of either voiding or ratifying it. For example, a contract for the sale of land which fails to mention that there is toxic waste on the property may be voidable by the purchaser.

More difficult is the nondisclosure situation. What if one party knows that the other would not agree to the contract if he were aware of all the facts? He doesn't have to disclose everything, but prior misrepresentations must be corrected. For example, a mistake in an offer cannot be snapped up by an offeree who wants to seize upon the error. Even if both parties were unaware of the mistake, the law will not enforce the contract if doing so would be "unconscionable" (that is, would cause undue surprise and hardship for one party). If *both* parties made a mistake about some fact that formed the basis of the bargain, the law will allow the person adversely affected to void the contract. The most famous example of this kind of mistake involved the sale of cotton to be delivered by the ship *Peerless* from Bombay. It turned out that there were two ships by that name, both sailing from Bombay but at different times, and each party had the other ship in mind. The court allowed the contract to be voided.

If there is a "fiduciary" relationship between the parties—where one of the parties has a legal duty to sacrifice his own interests to those of the other (e.g., trustees, guardians, and attorneys)—whatever facts are necessary to make a fully informed decision must be disclosed in advance. For example, a lawyer may not sell a piece of property to his financially strapped client without disclosing all the reasons his client should not buy it.

Legal Purpose

Courts will not enforce contracts between thieves and scoundrels for their illegal activities. But courts are more lenient if there is any way that one of the parties can be construed as a law-abiding citizen contracting for a legitimate purpose. For example, if Prettyboy promises to sell Badman a glass cutter knowing it is to be used in a burglary, the courts will enforce that contract. But if both parties are involved in the burglary, the courts will not consider them to have a legitimate creditor-debtor relationship.

Equity

Many agreements are "legally" unenforceable; lack of proper consideration and lack of a writing are probably the two most common reasons. Thus, gratuitous promises to give gifts, and oral promises to sell land are not "legally" enforceable. Nevertheless, there are many instances when it would be unfair *not* to enforce an agreement— primarily when one party relies on it and spends time or money in good faith reliance on the agreement.

Suppose a homeowner, offended by the sight of his lazy neighbor's unkempt property, promises orally to give his neighbor a $300 gift if he mows his lawn regularly. Even if the neighbor complies, he may not get the gift because in most jurisdictions there is a preexisting duty to maintain one's property. This is the time for what the law calls an "equitable remedy." The governing doctrine is called "promissory estoppel"—the purpose of which is to protect the promisee who in good faith relies on an otherwise unenforceable promise. (From the standpoint of legal strategy, an attorney would rather not have to use promissory estoppel because it focuses the court's attention on the reasonableness of the plaintiff's behavior—whether the plaintiff was reasonable in relying on the existence of an agreement.

It is easier to argue, for example, that the plaintiff's actions in reliance on the agreement were part of the bargain, that it represented his consideration in the contract.)

Equitable arguments rely on the same formula required of any other area of the law: the defendant owed the plaintiff a duty, which he breached, causing injury—and the plaintiff wants help. The doctrine of promissory estoppel tells the defendant: you can create a legally unenforceable duty by making a promise, but if someone reasonably relying on your promise is injured, he will have a cause of action against you. What makes promissory estoppel unique is that the injury occurs *before* the breach of duty—when the plaintiff acts to his detriment by spending time or money in reliance on the promise. In a sense, the injury *defines* the breach of duty.

Here's a famous case highlighting legal and equitable arguments. Sallydear receives a letter from her Uncle Will asking her to come take care of him: "If you sell your house and come live with me, I will leave you my farm." Sallydear sells her house and arrives on the farm to look after her Uncle Will. Soon thereafter he dies; there is no document other than the letter which indicates that Sallydear is entitled to the farm. She would prefer to argue that his offer was a conditional offer calculated to induce her to sell her house, part of a contractual bargain to live with him on the farm. Uncle Will's other heirs, who also stand ready to inherit the farm, argue that the offer was simply stating the obvious: that the niece would have to sell her house before she moved in.

For Sallydear to win, she must prove that Uncle Will breached a duty imposed on him by their "contract," enforceable because there was an offer, acceptance, and consideration on both sides. If the letter is construed as nothing more than a gratuitous gesture—unsupported by consideration on her part, she loses. Sallydear, however, can convert Uncle Will's gratuitous promise into a duty to perform by invoking the doctrine of promissory estoppel, if she can prove that she actually and reasonably believed her uncle would will her the farm, and that it was reasonable for her to sell her house in reliance on the promise (instead of, say, renting it).

Promissory estoppel is closely related to another equitable doctrine called quasi-contract. In both doctrines the plaintiff gives up valuable consideration in reliance upon an assumed agreement. Under promissory estoppel the plaintiff gives his consideration to a third party, whereas under quasi-contract he gives it directly to the defendant. Under promissory estoppel, the defendant expressly promises the plaintiff something. Under quasi-contract, however, no express promise is made, so the plaintiff must convince the court of the defendant's *implied* promise. Under quasi-contract, however, no express promise is made, so the plaintiff must convince the court of the defendant's *implied* promise. This argument often succeeds because it prevents unjust enrichment by the defendant. For instance, a nephew agrees to work for his uncle for the summer, in exchange for which the uncle agrees to pay his nephew's college tuition for the next semester. Before the summer is over, the uncle decides to sell his business and declines to pay the tuition. The nephew responds with a lawsuit, claiming that he should be paid for the work he performed because there was a quasi-contract; to do otherwise, he argues, would unjustly enrich the uncle.

The remedy under quasi-contract can be considerably different than under promissory estoppel, where a court may declare the contract fully enforceable. Under quasi-contract, the court will enforce a contract only up to the value of the consideration given the defendant. In the above example, the value of the consideration given the defendant was the value of the nephew's work until the business was sold.

Statute of Frauds

Some contracts must be in writing to be enforceable. Courts are skeptical that, on the basis of an oral agreement alone, someone would buy a piece of real property, guarantee another person's loan, or contract to do a project lasting more than a year. The UCC extends the writing requirement to all contracts involving goods over $500.

Modifications of agreements involving real estate, loan guarantees, and projects which cannot be performed in less than a year must also be in writing. Odd, but for other kinds of contracts governed by the common law the parties *cannot* agree to make all modifications in writing. The UCC is more deferential to the contracting parties; if the parties agree not to change the contract unless the change is in writing, the parties will be held to that agreement.

The writing necessary to satisfy the Statute of Frauds does not have to be fancy. It can even be pieced together through several correspondences. If a written intention cannot be pieced together, the plaintiff's lawyer must figure out some way to "remove" the contract from the Statute of Frauds. There are three major ways to do this: 1) by applying the law of equity—substantial performance, unequivocal reference, estoppel, and quasi-contract; 2) by the defendant's admission; or 3) under the UCC, acceptance or payment for goods that are unique, or when there is an "unanswered memo."

Statute of Frauds: Land Contracts

Contracts with real estate brokers do not need to be in writing to be enforceable; they are automatically excluded from the Statute of Frauds. But other sales of real property are well within the Statute. Suppose Bigbucks orally promises to sell an apartment building to Lowman, who makes a $4000 down payment—but Bigbucks doesn't deliver the deed, denying that he ever agreed to sell the building. If Lowman can prove that Bigbucks owed him a duty as set out in a written agreement, he can certainly prove that the breach injured him to the tune of $4000. If Bigbucks had written "down payment on apartment building" on Lowman's $4000 check, Lowman could argue that the check satisfies the writing requirement for the Statute of Frauds. (Without such a statement, however, a cancelled check alone won't prove an agreement because the court has no way of knowing why $4000 passed hands.) Without a writing, how is Lowman going to prove they had an enforceable contract? The best way would be to get Bigbucks to admit the contract under oath. Next best would be to get a third person to testify that Bigbucks told him of the sale.

In situations like this, when justice and fairness require, the law of equity may be imposed to declare a contract enforceable—if the plaintiff can show that he actually and reasonably relied on the agreement. That reliance may be "substantial performance," which in the case of a land sale means taking possession of the property (and, in some states, making improvements on it.)

If Lowman hasn't yet occupied the property, he can still prove to an equity court that there was a contract by introducing evidence of behavior by which Bigbucks unequivocally referred to their agreement. He may have put the apartment building's gas and electric bills in Lowman's name; he may have given notice of termination to his employees at the building; or he may have taken down a "For Sale" sign.

Statute of Frauds: Loan Guarantees

Promises to answer for the debts of another must also be in writing to be enforceable. A classic example is the surety agreement: a debtor borrows money from a creditor, and the debtor's friend promises to pay on the loan if the debtor fails to do so. The creditor still has to go to the debtor for repayment of the loan, but if he refuses to pay, the creditor can then look to the surety for the money.

The one exception to the writing requirement is if the suretor made the promise in order to benefit himself. Suppose that three months earlier Ne'erdowell had borrowed $1000 from Goodfriend to start a business. Trying to keep the business from going bankrupt, he returns for another loan, but Goodfriend tells him he has no more money to lend. Instead of losing any chance of being repaid, Goodfriend proposes a plan in which another creditor will lend the money, with Goodfriend agreeing to become a surety for the new loan. Such an agreement does not need to be in writing to be enforceable, because the reason Goodfriend agreed to become a surety was to protect his original $1000 loan, not to benefit the debtor.

If Goodfriend had made the same assurance to the debtor ("if you don't pay, I will"), instead of to the lender ("if he doesn't pay, I will"), he would be an indemnitor. Under a surety agreement, the lender must first seek repayment from the debtor before going after the surety. Under an indemnity agreement, only the debtor can look to the indemnitor for payment, because the indemnitor's promise was to the debtor and not to the creditor. Indemnity agreements are outside the Statute of Frauds, and therefore can be enforced without a writing.

Goodfriend could have gone one step further and guaranteed the loan—agreeing to let the creditor come after him for the money without first seeking payment from the debtor. But guarantees, like sureties, must be in writing. Or Goodfriend could have told the creditor to shift the entire debt to him. The debtor would no longer be responsible for the debt. This is called a "novation" and does *not* require a writing because the friend is no longer answering for the debt of another, but rather answering for his own debt (which he incurred by transferring the obligation to pay to himself).

Statute of Frauds: Contracts Which Cannot Be Performed Within One Year

The only tricky part of contracts lasting more than a year is that the year begins when the contract is signed—not when the work is begun. So if you contract to work for six months, with work to begin in seven months, that contract has to be in writing.

A strange result under the Statute of Frauds is that if you agree to work for someone for two years, that employment contract must be in writing because it cannot possibly be performed in one year. But if you contract to work for a lifetime, the contract does *not* have to be in writing because it's possible to perform the contract in less than one year (your lifetime could be less than one year).

Statute of Frauds: UCC

Under the UCC, any sale of goods valued at $500 or more must be in writing and contain both the essential terms of the offer and a signed acknowledgement that the parties are willing to be bound by the agreement.

As mentioned, the UCC honors a clause by which the parties agree that they will not modify their contract unless the modification is in writing. (The common law will not honor such clauses unless the modification concerns a transaction in land, a surety agreement, or a contract which cannot be performed in less than a year.)

It is easier to circumvent the Statute of Frauds if the contract concerns transactions in goods. Not only does the plaintiff have the same arguments he had under the common law (admission, substantial performance, unequivocal reference, estoppel, and quasi-contract), but under the UCC oral contracts for goods valued more than $500 are enforceable when the goods are unique, when they have been accepted by the buyer or payment has been accepted by the seller, and when a memo between merchants goes unanswered for ten days.

Unique goods are those that are so specially made that they cannot be resold to someone else (for example, goods engraved with the purchaser's name). Consequently, once the goods have been manufactured, it would be unfair to the seller not to enforce the contract, even though the agreement was never put in writing.

If the buyer accepts the goods, or if the seller accepts payment, each has implicitly admitted that there was a contract. If the buyer had received only part of the goods, the UCC will enforce the contract only up to the value of the goods actually accepted. Likewise for partial payment: without a writing to verify an agreement, the seller is only obligated to deliver goods actually paid for.

If one merchant sends a memo to another, whatever is in the memo will be held against him as an admission. In addition, the recipient will be bound to the memo if he doesn't object in writing within ten days. In other words, if a merchant places an order, he has a right to expect another merchant to fill that order. If the merchant seller doesn't deliver (or object within ten days), the law will hold him in breach. That's business.

Risk of Loss

Which party has the duty to pay for goods lost or destroyed through no fault of either? If neither party breached the contract, the risk of loss shifts from the seller to the buyer once the seller has delivered the goods to the place agreed upon. If the goods are being shipped, for example, the seller's obligation is to get the goods loaded onto the carrier. The buyer and seller can agree to change that obligation by changing the shipping contract into a "destination" contract. In that case, the seller's obligation is to get the goods to the destination point and tender the goods to the seller. If the goods are being sold at the seller's place of business and the seller is a merchant, the risk passes to the buyer when the buyer takes possession of the goods. If the seller is not a merchant, the risk passes a reasonable time after the seller has offered the goods to the buyer.

If one of the parties breaches the contract, the risk of loss is partially shifted to the breaching party for a period of time. If, for example, the buyer breaches and the goods are damaged within a reasonable time thereafter, the seller can hold the buyer liable for any damages not covered by the seller's insurance. If the buyer rightfully revokes his acceptance of non-conforming goods (goods not conforming to the terms of the agreement), and the goods are damaged within a reasonable time thereafter, the buyer can hold the seller liable for any damages not covered by the buyer's insurance.

In a shipment contract, if the seller breaches by delivering non-conforming goods to the carrier, and the goods are damaged in transit, the buyer can hold the seller liable for any damages not covered by the buyer's insurance.

Third-Party Beneficiaries

Up to this point in our discussion of contract law, the only parties to whom a duty of performance has been owed were the offeror and the offeree. Third parties can also have the power to demand performance; they are called "third-party beneficiaries." In third-party beneficiary contracts, A gives his consideration to B, but B gives his consideration to C, who becomes the third-party beneficiary.

A father promises a car dealer that he will pay him $10,000 to deliver a car to his daughter. The car dealer is the promisor and the father the promisee. The daughter is the intended third-party beneficiary; she has a claim only if she (a) learns about the promise and notifies both the promisor and promisee that she agrees to be a third-party beneficiary to their agreement, or (b) gives up valuable consideration in reliance on the promise. She is the *intended* third-party beneficiary because it is clear to whom the car dealer will give his consideration. If she were only an "incidental" beneficiary—one who benefits from the contract only as an indirect result of the promisor giving consideration to the promisee—she could not enforce the contract. Thus, if the father has told the car dealer to deliver the car to *him*, not to his daughter, she would be only an incidental beneficiary and could not sue to enforce the contract.

Some of the terminology in third-party beneficiary contracts can be confusing. If, for example, the daughter had already contracted with the dealer to buy the car, and the father says to him, "If my daughter doesn't pay, I will," the father becomes a surety for his daughter's debt. Thus, surety agreements can also be a type of third-party beneficiary contract: the promisor (car dealer) has already given his consideration (car) to the third-party beneficiary (daughter), and the promisee (father) is now promising to pay the promisor if the third-party beneficiary doesn't.

Had the father told his daughter, "If you don't pay, I will," he would be an *indemnitor* of his daughter's debt. If he had said to the car dealer, "I will pay whether or not my daughter pays," he would be a *guarantor* of the debt. Again, the difference: under a surety agreement, the creditor (car dealer) must first demand payment from the daughter before going after the father; under a guarantee arrangement, the creditor can go after the father without first having to demand payment from the daughter.

When you endorse a check, you become a surety for everyone who signed before you. The term for such a surety is "accommodation party." If the check was not made out or endorsed to you, but you endorse the back of the check anyway, you become a guarantor of the check, allowing whoever now owns the check to demand payment from you without first asking for payment from those who signed before you.

Pay to the Order of: **Carl Ellis**

One thousand dollars and no cents. . . . $1,000.00

Jack McPherson

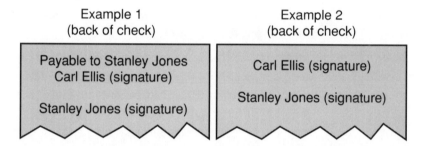

| Example 1 (back of check) | Example 2 (back of check) |

In example 1, Stanley Jones is a surety (accommodation party) for Carl Ellis. In example 2, Stanley Jones is a guarantor of the check because Carl Ellis did not endorse the check to Stanley Jones.

Warranties

Warranties present another cause of action—separate from breach of contract and torts—under which a duty is imposed on the seller to sell what he agreed to sell. An express warranty is a guarantee by the seller that the service or product he sells conforms to his own description of it, which could be oral, written, a sample, blueprints, or goods sent to the buyer in the past. Leeway is given for the salesman's opinions, sometimes called "puffing." The seller is also held to any express warranty given *after* the sale. Statements such as "This car can go eighty miles per hour, it gets twenty-five miles per gallon, and it has never been in an accident" are all express warranties.

The UCC demands that beyond selling what they say they are selling, merchants adhere to an "implied warranty of merchantability." This is a statutory duty to sell goods fit for the marketplace, which means that they must pass without objection in the trade, be adequately packaged and conform to statements on the label, and be fit for the ordinary purpose for which they are used.

A third warranty under the UCC is the "implied warranty of fitness for a particular purpose," which is given whenever the seller knows of the customer's particular needs, and the customer relies on the seller's knowledge in selecting the proper goods. The seller does not have to be a merchant, and the buyer does not have to tell the seller of his particular needs so long as the seller has reason to know of them and of the customer's reliance on the seller.

The seller can disclaim both an implied warranty of merchantability and an implied warranty of fitness for a particular purpose—but *not* an express warranty. The seller cannot disclaim what he has just given. (To protect himself from disagreements over what was promised, the seller can insert an "integration clause" into the contract, confirming that everything agreed to is included in the written contract, and that there are no outstanding oral agreements.) An implied warranty of merchantability can be disclaimed orally. If it is disclaimed in writing it must be conspicuously displayed and contain the word "merchant-ability." An implied warranty for a particular purpose can *only* be disclaimed in writing. While it must be conspicuous, it need not contain any specific words; "as is" or "with all faults" will do for a disclaimer. Many states limit a merchant's ability to disclaim either of the implied warranties when selling to lay consumers.

Torts

Like contracts, torts are a quilt of common and constitutional law, statutes, and equity. Tort law places duties on people to prevent them from injuring others or their property. In the absence of an agreed-upon relationship (a contract), the law of torts will impose a duty of performance if it finds a sufficient relationship between the parties. In other words, the duty of performance is triggered simply by the relationship between the parties. Thus, a doctor owes a duty to his patients, but not to the patient's friends.

The legal relationship (and duty) of a defendant employee to an injured plaintiff is often extended to include the defendant's employer—who is held "vicariously liable" for acts occurring on the job. Here the law calls the employee an "agent," and the employer a "principal." "On the job" means that the employee was where he was supposed to be, at a time when he was supposed to be there, and doing what he was supposed to be doing (or at least doing something to advance his boss' interest). Employers are not vicariously liable for tortious acts of independent contractors. Whether someone is an employee or an independent contractor depends, for the most part, on how much control the employer could exercise over the employee's work. Thus, the owner of a restaurant is not liable for negligent acts of the repairman whom he hired to fix the air conditioner—but he is responsible for the negligent acts of his waiter.

Our central question under Issue 1, again, is whether the defendant owed the plaintiff a duty to perform. In torts, the subissues involve the specific duty owed, under what circumstances that duty is imposed, and to whom it is owed—as outlined in the following causes of action.

INTENTIONAL TORTS AGAINST THE PERSON

If the plaintiff is:	And the defendant is:	Then the defendant owes the plaintiff a duty not to:
Anyone	Anyone	Assault him.
Anyone	Anyone	Commit battery against him.
Anyone	Anyone	Falsely imprison him.
Anyone	Anyone	Intentionally inflict severe emotional harm.
Anyone living	Anyone	Injure the plaintiff's reputation with defamatory falsehoods.

If the plaintiff is:	And the defendant is:	Then the defendant owes the plaintiff a duty not to:
Anyone	Anyone	Sue the plaintiff on frivolous grounds, or cause the plaintiff to be falsely prosecuted for a criminal offense.
Anyone	Anyone	Invade the plaintiff's privacy.

Intentional Torts Against The Person

Assault

Assault is any act which intentionally puts the plaintiff in anticipation of being imminently hurt or touched in some offensive manner. Example: aiming a gun at someone.

The "anticipation" of being hurt or offensively touched must be both actual and reasonable, meaning that the plaintiff must be aware of the assault from which a reasonable person would anticipate being hurt or offensively touched. (Hence, words alone are usually not an assault.) Aiming a gun at someone's back is not an assault unless the victim is actually aware of the threat, nor is assailing someone with a floppy rubber knife—because there is no reasonable anticipation of being harmed. Whether the defendant was actually capable of harming or offending the plaintiff is irrelevant so long as the plaintiff reasonably believed that the defendant intended to do so. The plaintiff does not have to prove that he was in fear, only that he *anticipated* being hurt. (The phrase "anticipation of being hurt" is used instead of "fear of being hurt" to prevent the defendant from claiming that the plaintiff could easily have escaped or defended himself, and hence was not in fear.)

Battery

Battery is any unpermitted and intentionally harmful or offensive contact regardless of whether the victim was aware of the contact. Under the proper circumstances, slapping or fondling or spitting at someone can all qualify as harmful or offensive contact. The plaintiff has the burden of proving that the act was unpermitted—that is, there was a lack of consent. To determine whether consent was given (express, implied, or apparent), a court must determine whether the plaintiff had authority to give consent; whether it was given voluntarily; whether it was informed (based on knowledge of material facts); and what the scope of the consent was.

In batteries, the defendant's motive is irrelevant. What is important is not why he struck the defendant, but whether he intended to do so. Just because the defendant thought the plaintiff liked being slapped on the back while drinking beer does not excuse the act if a judge or jury deems such an act harmful or offensive.

Intent is not always easy to prove. Someone might do something *realizing* that harm could occur without actually *intending* injury. The line is crossed when the likelihood of harming another becomes a substantial certainty.

False Imprisonment

False imprisonment, being an intentional tort, requires proof that the defendant intentionally tried to restrict the plaintiff's freedom of movement without his consent. Like battery, motive is irrelevant. To be falsely confined, the plaintiff must be aware of his confinement and have no reasonable way of escaping to freedom. Thus, a patient may have a valid claim of false imprisonment if kept in the hospital against his wishes.

Intentional Infliction of Emotional Distress

To sue under this cause of action, the plaintiff must prove that the defendant's actions would be outrageous to a reasonable person, and that the emotional distress was severe and accompanied by physical manifestations like insomnia, depression, and loss of appetite.

Defamation

Tort law imposes a duty not to spread false and defamatory information about living people. Defamation occurs when the defendant makes a false and defamatory statement about the plaintiff to a third person. Defamatory statements made in writing are called libel; those made orally are called slander.

A statement is defamatory if the plaintiff's reputation is actually and reasonably damaged in the minds of a substantial and respectable segment of the community. The defamatory statement cannot be merely an opinion; it must be a statement of fact, and it must actually and reasonably refer to the plaintiff. The mayor cannot sue you for stating that "all politicians are crooked." Even falsely claiming that "Black Jack stole my Harley Davidson" may not be libelous if Black Jack's friends and acquaintances have not changed their attitudes about him. A defendant who *negligently* defames a third person may be as liable as if he had done so intentionally.

The plaintiff has the burden of proving the statement false if he is a public figure or if the issue being litigated is a matter of public concern. The burden shifts to the defendant to prove the statement true if the plaintiff is a private figure suing over a non-newsworthy event. Claiming that the president of a road-building company bribed the mayor to secure a contract places the burden on the president to prove the allegation false at trial, but claiming that the president of the company embezzled money from his company places the burden to prove the allegation true upon the person making the claim.

The United States Constitution guarantees a free press. Allowing plaintiffs to sue the media for every innocent but defamatory statement would soon jeopardize an important Constitutional freedom. For this reason, when the press is the defendant, the Supreme Court requires a private plaintiff to prove that the press should have checked its facts before publishing false and defamatory statements about his private life—a negligence standard. An even higher, intentional standard is required when the plaintiff is a public figure who can command his own press outlets to rebut the press' charges. Public figures must prove that the defendant published false and defamatory statements *knowing* they were false and defamatory or at least with serious doubts about their truth. The same is true for private figures alleging defamation concerning a matter of public concern.

The law does not allow a dead person's family to sue for defamation on his or her behalf.

Malicious Prosecution and Abuse of Process

Tort law prohibits us from harassing a person by instituting litigation against him without reasonable cause, or by falsely supplying the state with facts that precipitate criminal proceedings. In order to sue for malicious prosecution, the plaintiff must be found innocent, or the charges must be dropped. Thus the ex-wife who falsely informs the IRS of her ex-husband's tax evasion may be liable for malicious prosecution. The tort known as abuse of process protects people from harassment by frivolous court proceedings initiated out of vengence.

Invasion of Privacy

Tort law distinguishes damage to reputation (defamation) from damage to privacy. These constitute two separate causes of action. One's private life is protected by the law from physical intrusion, public disclosure, "false light," and commercial use.

Physical intrusion includes such acts as secret photographs, eavesdropping, and trespass, even if the information obtained is not made public.

The kinds of things protected from public disclosure are those private matters which a reasonable person would find highly embarrassing if made public, and which are of no legitimate concern to the public. This does not include matters of public record, which are not protected from nosey and inconsiderate intruders.

"False light" invasion of privacy occurs when someone (usually for commercial reasons) intentionally or recklessly makes an untruthful but believable statement which injures a person's reputation. One difference between false light invasion of privacy and defamation is that under false light the injury to reputation is milder and more indirect; a bigger difference is the interest intruded upon. With defamation, a person's reputation is maligned; with false light, his privacy

INTENTIONAL TORTS AGAINST THE PLAINTIFF'S REAL
AND PERSONAL PROPERTY

If the plaintiff is:	And the defendant is:	Then the defendant owes the plaintiff a duty not to:
Landowner	Anyone	Trespass on his property.
Landowner	Anyone	Interfere with the Landowner's use of his property (Nuisance).
Owner	Anyone	Steal or interfere with his personal property (Conversion).
Contracting party	The other contracting party	Misrepresent material facts.
One party to a contract	Anyone	Cause the other party to the contract to breach his contractual obligations to the plaintiff.
Anyone likely to receive an economic benefit	Anyone	Use fraud, duress, or undue influence to prevent the plaintiff from receiving that economic benefit.

invaded. A libelous statement that draws attention from the press may also support a claim for false light invasion of privacy.

People also have a right not to have their names, faces, and reputations used for commercial purposes without their permission. A person's privacy may be invaded even though such use might enhance a person's reputation. For example, the Coca Cola company cannot photograph Bo Jackson drinking a Coke and use that picture without his permission.

Intentional Torts Against Real and Personal Property

Trespass to Land

Trespass is the intentional interference with another's right to exclusive possession of his land. The plaintiff does not have to own the land to sue for trespass. A lessee, for example, can sue a trespasser because, as lessee, he has the right to exclusive possession. An apartment dweller can even sue his landlord for trespass if the landlord has no right to be in the apartment at that moment.

Trespass includes any entry onto another's land—either by the defendant himself, his equipment, or objects flung by the defendant onto the plaintiff's property. Rocks dumped off a cliff onto the plaintiff's property constitutes trespass, but less tangible events—like smoke or heat wafting onto the plaintiff's property—may require the plaintiff to sue under a claim of nuisance.

Intentional does not mean the defendant intended to trespass, only that he intended to do the act which happened to constitute trespass. The intent to trespass would be the motive for doing the culpable act. (Culpable is to civil law what guilty is to criminal law.) Thus, the defendant is liable for trespass if he intended to drive his car onto the plaintiff's property.

Nuisance

Whereas trespass is the interference with another's possession of his land, nuisance is the interference with another's use and enjoyment of his land. Nuisance actions are usually reserved for intangible things—like noise, light, or odors—that cross onto plaintiff's property. Whether something is a nuisance depends on the reasonableness of the defendant's activity; courts look at the feasibility of the defendant's alternative choices, and balance the harm which could be avoided against the social benefit of the defendant's actions. For example, if the court finds that an airport has no alternative flight paths it may deny a claim for nuisance by those living in the area.

If the defendant's activity is causing a *public* nuisance, only the state can sue to enjoin it. A private party has a cause of action only if the nuisance is affecting him in a way different from everyone else. Thus, a private party can sue a company polluting a stream by showing that his is the only business being adversely affected.

Conversion

Conversion is the civil equivalent of theft, in which the defendant takes possession (dominion) or exercises control over the plaintiff's personal property. Mere interference with such property is called "trespass to chattel."

Misrepresentation

In general, misrepresentation must be of a material fact, not of the law (because all of us are presumed to know the law). In most cases the defendant must have known that what he was misrepresenting was false, and have intended to deceive the plaintiff. Stricter courts require more than good faith (empty-headed) reliance on the defendant's statements, granting relief only if a reasonable person would also have relied on the misrepresentation. This allows a seller to give his sales pitch without fear that the buyer will hold the seller to his puffing. Negligent misrepresentation, which lacks the element of "intent to deceive," is also actionable, but the plaintiff must have been foreseeable by the defendant as someone who might be hurt by his misrepresentation.

Interference with Contractual Relations

Once a contract is signed, the parties are protected by tort law from anyone interfering and encouraging one of the parties to breach. Thus, one company cannot induce a competitor's employees with financial enticements to breach their long-term contracts.

Interference with Advantageous Relations

This cause of action typically arises when a person—using fraud, duress, or undue influence—intentionally persuades a testator to cut someone out of his will.

NEGLIGENT TORTS

If the plaintiff is:	And the defendant is:	Then the defendant owes the plaintiff a duty not to:
Foreseeable	Anyone	Negligently injure him.
Foreseeable	Anyone	Negligently cause his death (wrongful death action).
Victim of emergency	The one who created the emergency	Stand by without helping.
Patient	Doctor	Omit material facts to make an informed decision about diagnostic tests and treatment; practice medicine below standards set by the medical profession.
Business invitee	Landowner	Fail to inspect the land for hazards and remove them.
Social guest	Landowner	Fail to remove known hazards on the property (no duty to inspect for hazards).
Licensee	Landowner	Same as social guest.
Trespasser	Landowner	Build especially dangerous hazards intended to keep trespassers off the land.
Frequent trespasser	Landowner	Fail to warn of known dangers on the land.
Discovered trespasser	Landowner	Fail to use reasonable care to avoid injuring him.
Infant trespasser	Landowner	Fail to remove hazards when landowner knows children come onto his property.

If the plaintiff is:	And the defendant is:	Then the defendant owes the plaintiff a duty not to:
Victim in sudden dire need of help	Potential rescuer	No duty owed, unless defendant created the emergency or had a legal duty to rescue the plaintiff (parent-child, lifesaver-swimmer, landowner-business invitee, social guest, licensee, and in most jurisdictions, trespassers).
Policeman or fireman	Landowner	Same as social guest.

Negligent Torts

Each of us has a duty not to expose others to unreasonable risks. Whether a risk was unreasonable under the circumstances is determined by a jury. In technical situations—medical malpractice, for example—the courts often ask an expert whether the defendant exposed the plaintiff to unreasonable risks.

The law is riddled with the term "reasonable." What makes one choice reasonable and another not is determined by the risk associated with each choice balanced against things like the urgency of the problem and the technical feasibility, cost, and social benefit of each choice. Risk is measured by a famous formula announced by Judge Learned Hand: the likelihood that harm will occur multiplied by the degree of harm. For example, an ophthalmologist examines a young woman complaining of failing vision. Because glaucoma is such a rare disease in young people, the ophthalmologist opts not to measure her intraocular pressures. Over the next year, her vision deteriorates to the point of legal blindness. In the ensuing lawsuit, it was determined that although the likelihood of glaucoma was low, the degree of harm was high, making the risk of glaucoma fairly substantial. Considering that measurement of intraocular pressure is such a simple, low risk, low cost procedure, the ophthalmologist's failure to do so exposed the plaintiff to an unreasonable risk, constituting a breach of the standard of due care owed her.

As another example, nuclear energy has a low likelihood of causing harm but a potentially high degree of harm in case of a meltdown. Nuclear power is technologically feasible, but it comes with a considerable price tag. For society, is the trade-off of having acid-free rain and a source of energy independent of the Middle East worth the risk of nuclear contamination? Compare nuclear energy with all other energy sources, and you will understand how difficult determining reasonableness can be.

The "wrongful death" statute gives the family of the deceased the right to sue the wrongdoer for damages suffered as a result of the loss of the family member. (A Survival Statute allows the family of the deceased to pursue any lawsuits the deceased had a right to institute or continue at the time of his death. Any awards go into the deceased's estate to be divided up among the creditors.) Damages may include loss of support, consortium, or companionship—but usually not pain and suffering incurred by the survivors.

Strict Liability

The concept of strict liability allows the plaintiff to hold a defendant liable for his injuries without having to prove he was negligent. Strict liability is applied when the defendant exposes the public to an abnormal danger which the defendant knew or should have known about.

The classic defendant in strict liability cases is an owner of a wild animal, but even owners of domestic animals are held strictly liable if they knew or should have known that the animal in question was dangerous. (e.g., a pit bull that had bitten three people the month before attacking the plaintiff).

Strict liability is also applied to anyone carrying on an abnormally dangerous activity—determined by the degree and likelihood that harm might occur, whether a safer method could have been used at reasonable expense without sacrificing benefit to the public, and whether the activity was particularly unusual for that locality.

Manufacturers, distributors, and retail outlets are strictly liable for their unreasonably dangerous products. What makes a product unreasonably dangerous is a defect in the product—either a design defect, making all the items defective, a manufacturing defect, making only that one item defective, or a failure to warn of risks associated with the product. Whether a design is unreasonably dangerous depends on the feasibility of designing a safer model without destroying the usefulness of the product. For example, there is no way to reduce the danger of a knife without destroying its utility.

If the defect caused the injury, then any foreseeable plaintiff injured by the product may sue under strict liability as long as he used the product in a foreseeable manner. Foreseeable plaintiffs include the purchasers, the users, the consumers, and even bystanders and rescuers. Foreseeable uses of the product may extend beyond reasonable uses.

Retail outlets that receive the product in a closed container and then simply sell the container are protected from strict liability suits. For example, a computer store receives equipment from the manufacturer and installs it own software on the hard drive before selling the unit to the public. One such computers causes a serious electrical injury to a purchaser. Because the store had opened the manufacturer's container to alter the computer, it may now be liable (along with the manufacturer) for the injury.

REAL PROPERTY

In the law of real property the event that establishes a legal relationship between two parties is an interest in land. Much of property law is concerned with defining the exact nature of that interest, which in turn defines the rights and duties of the owner. It is important, therefore, to know how the property interest is established. The following charts help summarize these points. (Don't expect to memorize the charts now. Use the charts to help pigeonhole the material presented in your real property course. Because concurrent estates are particularly susceptible to being destroyed without intent to do so, pay particular attention to how concurrent estate are destroyed, and to what happens thereafter.)

POSSESSORY ESTATES

Interest	How Created	Rights and Duties	If Contingency Occurs
Present Interests			
Absolute			
Fee Simple	To A		
	Adverse possession[1]		
Life estate	To A for Life	Rights:	If A dies, estate goes to grantor or remainderman[2]
		Possession (including right to all rents and profits, and right to evict anyone from the property); *Enjoyment* (including right to use and enjoy the property without the property being damaged by others; *Alienation* (including the right to lease, sell, or mortgaged his interest in the property); *Fixtures* (including the right to remove his personal property from the property, provided the removal does not permanently damage the property).	
		Duties:	
		Pay taxes; pay off any mortagage he obtains on the property; not to commit waste.[3]	
Estate for years	To A for X years	(Landlord-Tenant[4]) The landlord owes his tenant all duties agreed upon in the lease agreement, plus: give the tenant the "right" to immediate possession,[5] disclose any defects the tenant would	After X years, reverts to grantor
Periodic estate	No fixed termination date, e.g., "from month to month"		

not reasonably discover (latent defects); not interfere with the tenant's quiet enjoyment of the property.[6] For residential premises, inspect and maintain the property in compliance with local health and safety codes,[7] inspect the property for hazards and repair them.[8] For multiunit dwellings, maintain and repair the areas under his control—the "common areas" (stairwells, elevators, lobby, etc.). The tenant owes his landlord all duties agreed upon in the lease agreement, plus: a duty not to damage the property above reasonable wear and tear. The tenant owes a duty to his guests to protect them from hazards on the property even when the tenant has no duty to repair the hazard.

Qualified		
Determinable estate	To A "so long as," "until," or "during"	Reverts to grantor (possibility of reverter)
Estate subject to condition subsequent		Grantee retains possessory rights until grantor takes steps to revest title to the property

Interest	How Created	Rights and Duties	If Contingency Occurs
Estate subject to executory limitation	To A, but if X happens, to B and his heirs		If X happens, B gets the property in fee simple (B has a shifting executory interest)
Future Interests Reversionary Possibility of reverter	To A "so long as," "until," or "during"		
Right of reentry	To A but grantor retains right to take back the estate if contingency occurs		
Nonreversionary Vested remainder	To A for life, then to B[9] "To my sons," at my death		
Vested remainder subject to open[10]			
Vested remainder subject to complete divestment[11]	To A for life, then to B, but if B dies without children, to C and his heirs		

Contingent remainder[12]	To A for life, then to B if B outlives A	If B does not outlive A, the property reverts back to grantor
Shifting executory interest[13]	To A, but if X happens, to C and his heirs	
Springing executory interest[14]	To A for life, then to B one year after A's death. To A for life, then to heirs of C.	During the year after A's death, the property reverts to grantor. At the time of A's death, if C is still alive, (i.e., no heirs of C identified yet), A's heirs take a reversionary interest until C dies. At C's death, C's heirs can exercise their springing executory interest and take the property.

1. Adverse possession is a means by which a person can get title to property simply by possessing the land continuously for a long time—at common law, 20 years. The possession must be without the owner's permission ("hostile"), at a time when the owner knew, or should have known, of the possession. The adverse possessor need not know that he was on the land without permission, but his occupation must be "notorious" enough that, to a reasonable person, the adverse possessor was acting as the owner of the land. This means that the adverse possessor cannot share the land with the true owner. On the other hand, if the land is only used by the true owner in the summertime, the adverse possessor need only possess the land in the summertime.

2. The holder of a future interest is called a remainderman.

3. Waste is any act or omission that reduces the property value more than expressly or impliedly permitted by the grantor, or more than is reasonable.

4. The duties owed to one another by landlords and tenants are governed by a mixture of common law, statutory law, and contract law.

5. The right to immediate possession does not mean the landlord has to deliver the vacant property to the tenant. If the previous tenant holds over, the new tenant—not the landlord—has the obligation to evict the holdover tenant.

6. If the landlord evicts the tenant, the tenant does not have to pay rent. "Constructive" eviction occurs when the landlord breaches his duty (covenant) not to interfere with the tenant's use and enjoyment of the property, or allows anyone under his control to interfere.

7. The landlord's duty to maintain the property in compliance with local health and safety codes cannot be waived by the tenant.

8. The landlord does not have to make repairs on damage intentionally done by the tenant.

9. Because B's interest is vested, if B is dead at A's death, B's heirs inherit the interest granted to B.

10. Vested remainders subject to open are subject to the "Rule Against Perpetuities, a rule that voids a person's nonreversionary future interest if his interest does not vest within 21 years after the death of a member of a class of people living at the time of creation of the person's interest. Creation of the interest occurs at the time of transfer of title to the grantee, or death of the grantor, if the transfer is by a will. The sequence of events, then, is death of the grantor (or transfer of title), death of the measuring life, and then 21 years:

The "Rule Against Perpetuities" applies when the measuring life is unborn, or the measuring life is a member of a class, some of whose members are unborn. Any possible creation of the measuring life, or possible creation of a new measuring life, after the creation of the interest could extend the time required to vest beyond the required 21 years from the time of death of the measuring life and thus violate the Rule Against Perpetuities. The Rule Against Perpetuities also applies when vesting occurs on the happening of a contingency that may not occur within 21 years of the death of the measuring life.

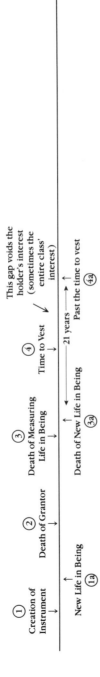

11. Grantee will take the property but lose it if a condition subsequent is fulfilled.
12. Grantee can only take the property if a condition precedent is met.
13. The contingency cannot be within the control of the grantor.
14. The grantee does not take possession of the property from the grantor until some future time.

Shared Estates

Joint Tenants

To create a joint tenancy, the agreement must explicitly state that there is a right of survivorship. There must be unity of title, unity of time, unity of interest (the most important unity), and unity of possession.

A joint tenancy is terminated with:

- Conveyance of, or contract to convey, one cotenant's interest.
- Mortgaging the property by one cotenant (in a title theory state).
- In some states, leasing one cotenant's interest.
- Judgment in a partition action.

Right of survivorship is destroyed for the interest conveyed or mortgaged. The owner of the severed piece is now a tenant-in-common with the other cotenants (who remain joint tenants to each other for the unsevered piece).

The rights of each party are as follows:

- Right of survivorship if another cotenant dies (at the death of a joint tenant, his interest passes to the other joint tenants, not to his estate).
- Right to alienate his interest.
- Right to use the whole property.
- Right to sue for partition from other cotenants.
- Right to lease his interest.
- Right to an accounting from other cotenants (each cotenant is entitled to receive fair rental income from his share of the property, but any more must be shared with the cotenants).

Tenants by the Entirety

To create a tenancy by the entirety, the parties must be married. Usually, tenants by the entirety is presumed if the property is taken by a married couple.

A tenancy by the entirety is terminated if the property is devised, the marriage is terminated by annulment or divorce, or the parties agree to change to another form of joint tenancy. Once terminated, the property is held as tenants-in-common.

The rights of each party are as follows:

- Right of survivorship, which is inalienable by either party alone.
- Each party's interest in the property is unattachable by judgment creditors unless the judgment is against the couple.
- Right to possess the whole property.

Tenants-in-Common

Where the tenants are in common, there is no right of survivorship, but the property is alienable, divisable, and leasable. The tenants have the right to possession of the whole property, as well as the right to partition it.

Buyer-Seller

To prove that there is a buyer-seller relationship, the common law—through the Statute of Frauds—requires that any conveyance (or promise of conveyance) of an interest in property be in a signed writing.

There must be a valid contract to convey the property interest. The agreement must be in writing (or pieced together from several writings), identifying the parties and property, evidencing an intent to sell (not lease or grant an easement or license), stating the price agreed upon (the courts will not enforce a "reasonable" price if no price was agreed upon), and signed by the party accused of defaulting.

- The seller must deliver a valid deed—signed by the seller, containing the name of the buyer, a description of the property being conveyed, and words indicating an intent to convey the interest. (Delivery does not mean physically giving the deed to the buyer. Mailing the deed or giving it to a neutral third party will suffice as long as the interest being relinquished by the seller to the buyer is immediate and irrevocable.)

- The seller must also warrant to the buyer or grantee that he has title to and possession of the property being conveyed (this and the following warranties pertain to general warranty deeds. Quit-claim deeds contain no warranties, and thus make no representation about the title.); that he has the right to convey the property; that there are no liens, mortgages, easements, or other encumbrances on the property; that the buyer, grantee, or successors in interest will not be disturbed in their enjoyment of the property by the grantor or by someone with claims of title superior to the buyer's or grantee's title; and that his title is good and that he will help defend against legal actions claiming superior title.

- The law of equity, through the doctrine of "equitable conversion," treats the buyer who has not yet taken possession nevertheless as the owner of the property. Thus, the seller has a duty to maintain the property in reasonable repair until the purchaser takes possession at closing. If the seller dies before the buyer is allowed to take possession, duties are imposed upon the seller's heirs to convey the property, and upon the buyer to pay the heirs the purchase price. Likewise, if the buyer dies before taking possession, the transaction must still proceed.

- At closing, the seller must provide marketable title—one which a reasonably knowledgeable businessman would accept. There must be no gaps in the chain of title, and it must purport to convey what was agreed upon, and be free of liens, restrictions (other than zoning), and easements that might interfere with the use of the property.

Duties of the Buyer:

- If the buyer learns of a defect in the title, he must notify the seller to allow the seller time to clear the defect.

- The doctrine of equitable conversion imposes a duty on the buyer to pay for any damage to the property occurring before the buyer takes possession. Any insurance proceeds paid to the seller for the damage go to the buyer.

Nonpossessory Property Interests

Easements

An easement is a right to use another's land. Public utility easements, for example, allow the electric company access to a homeowner's transformer and power lines. If use of the easement benefits the adjoining property, the easement is called an "appurtenant easement," and the property benefitted is the "dominant" estate; the burdened property is the "servient" estate. If use of the easement benefits a particular person, the easement is called an "easement in gross." Appurtenant easements allow anyone to use the easement as long as they do so to benefit the dominant estate. Appurtenant easements are automatically transferred with the servient and dominant estates. Easesments in gross cannot be alienated or devised.

An easement may be created:

• By an *an express writing*.

• By *unwritten implication*, as long as (1) the dominant and servient estates were once held in common ownership, (2) the owner of the servient estate knew or should have known that the parcel of land in question was being used on a regular basis as if it were an easement, and (3) the continued use of the parcel in question is reasonably necessary to the enjoyment of the dominant estate. In other words, having once used the parcel in question as an easement, the owner of the servient estate is deemed to have sold the dominant estate with the intent of continuing the "easement."

• By *necessity*, which commonly occurs when a large parcel of land is subdivided, leaving a landlocked parcel in the middle. The easement is strictly necessary for the access to the landlocked parcel (dominant estate). There is no writing requirement and no need to show that the owner used the parcel in question as an easement prior to subdivision. The necessity for the easement must have existed at the time of the subdivision. Easements in gross cannot be created by necessity.

• By *prescription*, which (like adverse possession) requires that the owner of the servient estate have actual knowledge, or objective knowledge (should have known), of people using his property without his permission, and that the use be continuous (or seasonal if that is how the easement is normally used) for as long as the statute of limitations requires (usually 20 years). But unlike adverse possession, the person using the easement need not exclude the owner of the servient estate from the easement area. For example, a property owner cannot begin to exclude skiers from crossing his property to get to the ski slope if they have been doing so with his knowledge for the past twenty years.

The easement holder must not use the easement to benefit land other than the dominant estate; not "overburden" the easement by using it for purposes never intended by the original owners; and maintain the easement in reasonable repair.

Appurtenant easements last forever unless actively terminated in one of the following ways:

1. By any *attempt* by the owner of the dominant estate *to sell* an appurtenant estate separately; by a *written release* from the owner of the easement; by *implication*—failure to use the easement plus some affirmative act indicating abandonment of the easement; by *merger* of the dominant and servient estates; by *prescription*—the owner of the servient estate prevents the owner of the easement from using the easement until the statute of limitations expires; or by *destruction* of the servient estate.

2. Easements by grant must be recorded by the easement holder; failure to do so will extinguish the easement if the servient estate is sold to a bona fide purchaser (one without knowledge of the easement). This does not apply to easements by implication, prescription, or necessity. Easements by necessity terminate when the necessity that prompted the easement no longer exists. Thus, if the state builds a road giving the landlocked property access to other roads, the easement by necessity automatically terminates.

3. The law of equity can be invoked to terminate an easement where the owner of the easement terminates it orally or fails to use the easement for a long time—both legally insufficient by themselves to

terminate the easement—and the owner of the servient estate relies to his detriment on the oral statement. For example, the easement owner erects a building on the property that would be too expensive to dismantle.

Licenses

Like easements in gross, licenses grant temporary permission to particular persons to cross the servient estate, but unlike easements in gross, licenses can be created outside the Statute of Frauds (no writing necessary) and can be terminated at the will of the licensor.

When a landowner revokes a license, the licensee can sue for damages, but not for permission to enter the land—unless the landowner is still allowing the licensee to keep his personal property on the land, or the landowner promised the licensee long-term use of the land and the licensee, acting reasonably, spent a lot of money in reliance on that promise.

Profits

Profits allow a person to enter another's land and take something from it (such as trees, crops, or water). There are appurtenant profits (if the appurtenant estate is benefitted) and profits in gross (if a particular person is benefitted by the profits). Thus removing water from a lake to irrigate a neighboring property is an appurtenant profit, while removing minerals for future sale is profits in gross. Unlike easements in gross, profits in gross are assignable to others.

Covenants

Covenants impose duties on one landowner to another without either ever having made any promises to each other. The duty stems from an agreement made between prior landowners. Farmer A and Farmer B agree that for a sum of money A will build an artificial lake for the use of B and all subsequent owners of B's property. Subsequent owners of A's property must allow use of the lake to all subsequent owners of B's property. Without ever having agreed to abide by the original agreement, each subsequent landowner—when he receives his interest in the property—also assumes the duties imposed by the original agreement, so long as the covenant (promise) "runs with the land." For this to happen, the original agreement must have been enforceable, in writing, signed by the promisor (acceptance of a deed containing the covenant will do), intended to run with the land, and "touch and concern" the land by physically or (in most jurisdictions) monetarily benefitting the promisee's land, or burdening the promisor's land, or both. In the example above, the promise to build the lake burdened A's property and benefitted B's. Had A agreed to build the lake without allowing B to use it, A's property would have been burdened without benefitting B's property.

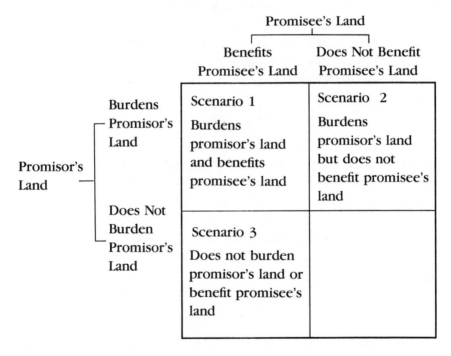

Scenario 1

The original promise benefitted the Promisee's land and burdened the Promisor's land. Successors in interest to the Promisee's land can sue the Promisor and the successors in interest to the Promisor's land.

Scenario 2

The original promise benefitted the Promisee's land but did not burden the Promisor's land. The successor in interest to the Promisee's land can sue the Promisor but not the successors in interest to the Promisor's land.

Scenario 3

The original promise did not benefit the Promisee's land but did burden the Promisor's land. Only the original Promisee can sue the successor in interest to the Promisor's land; successors in interest to the Promisee's land can sue neither the Promisor nor the successors in interest to the Promisor's land.

In other words, if the covenant benefits the Promisee's land without burdening the Promisor's land, or the covenant burdens the Promisor's land without benefitting the Promisee's land, successors in interest to the Promisee's land cannot impose a duty on the successors in interest to the Promisor's land to abide by the covenant.

Covenants either "run at law," meaning the plaintiffs can sue for money damages, or "run at equity," meaning the plaintiff can sue for specific performance or injunction. To run at law, a covenant (in addition to being a signed, written, enforceable agreement manifesting an intent to run with the land, that touches and concerns the land) must have horizontal and vertical "privity." That is, the promisor must have made his promise in the deed or lease—"horizontal privity"— and each successor to the promisor's and promisee's property must have obtained the property in some way other than by adverse possession or a foreclosure sale—"vertical privity."

To run at equity as an "equitable servitude," a covenant must (like a covenant running at law) be a signed, written, enforceable agreement manifesting an intent to run with the land, and touch and concern the land. But unlike covenants running at law, equitable servitudes are still enforceable by successors to the promisee against successors to the promisor even when the promise is not written into the deed or lease—so long as the successors to the promisee have vertical privity. In other words, even adverse possessors of the promisor's land or purchasers at a foreclosure sale still owe a duty to everyone in vertical privity with the promisee's property. Only a bona fide purchaser purchasing the promisor's land without actual, reasonable, or constructive notice of the equitable servitude can escape the duty owed to successors of the promisee's property.

Successors to one parcel of land can impose a duty on successors to another parcel if both are part of a "common scheme" of development—like a subdivision. What must be shown is that the developer imposed a similar set of restrictions on a reasonable number of lots in the subdivision before the lot in question was sold, so that later purchasers had notice of a common scheme restricting the use of their property. Since each lot owner in the common scheme owes a duty to every other lot owner, any lot owner can enforce the restrictions on any other.

Did the Defendant Fail to Perform?

Contracts

Before you can answer *whether* the defendant failed to perform, you have to know *what* the defendant was obligated to do. Under common law, the terms of the contract are the same as those made in the offer. Under the UCC, the contract terms include those in the offer, plus any additional (not different[1]) terms included in the acceptance, as long as the offeror and offeree were both merchants and the additional terms were not objected to by the offeror. In everyday commerce, there is usually no formal contract because the UCC has done away with the need to make a contract for every sale of goods. It did this by defining through statute the duties owed by the seller and buyer.

The seller under the UCC has the obligation to deliver conforming goods to a carrier and, if he agreed to deliver the goods to the buyer's place of business, arranging proper transport. The buyer has the obligation of discovering any readily apparent defects in the goods within a reasonable time after delivery, notifying the seller, and holding defective goods until the seller sends instructions for return or disposal. If asked, the buyer must list the defects in writing. The buyer is given

---

1. Different terms alter existing terms in the contract; additional terms do not.

a longer time to discover latent defects, but since he already accepted the goods, any latent defect serious enough to permit return must substantially impair the value of the goods—a stricter standard than simple non-conformance (the standard that allowed the buyer to reject the goods on delivery). For example, a defective emission-control will not allow you to return an automobile, but a defective set of piston rings will.

Accord and Satisfaction

In defending against a breach of contract action, the defendant is obviously going to deny that he failed to perform. He may put up a factual defense, claiming the plaintiff is mistaken about the defendant's acts, or he may put up a legal defense, claiming the plaintiff is mistaken about the duty imposed on him by the contract. He may, for example, deny that the goods were delivered to the wrong store, or assert that the contract allowed delivery to any one of the chain's outlets.

One commonly raised legal defense is "accord and satisfaction." What happens is this: the parties disagree about whether one of them breached and they try to resolve the situation themselves. They can either rescind their original contract and substitute a second one, or they can make the rescission of the original contract *contingent* on performance of the second. In the latter solution, if one of the parties does not perform the second contract, then the other party can sue for breach of either the original or the second contract. But if both parties do perform, then neither can sue for breach of the original agreement. The latter solution is called accord and satisfaction. The second (contingent) agreement is the accord, and performance of that agreement is the satisfaction. The defendant would defend the breach of contract claim by proving that he satisfied the accord. Since an accord and satisfaction is itself a contract, it must be supported by new consideration. Thus, when an automobile dealer fails to deliver the car ordered, the customer can agree to accept the wrong car for a lesser purchase price.

Anticipatory Breach

Just as the offeror does not have to wait for the offeree's performance to know that he has accepted—words of acceptance will do—neither party has to wait until performance is due to find out that the other party is *not* going to perform. Words of repudiation will suffice to cancel a contract even though performance is not yet due. The only exception is with unilateral contracts (which can *only* be accepted by performance), where words of repudiation are meaningless.

Not every concern voiced by the defendant can be construed as an "anticipatory breach." The words have to be a clear and definite repudiation of the contract—not, for example, a desire to renegotiate the contract. Acts which make performance impossible will also suffice for an anticipatory breach. If, after concluding a deal to sell his house, the owner turns around and sells it to someone else, he has anticipatorily repudiated the first sales contract.

A repudiation is like an offer. Once the repudiation is accepted or (under equity) detrimentally relied upon, the repudiating party cannot change his mind. Of course, the other party does not have to accept the repudiation: he can ignore it and hope that the repudiator will change his mind. If he does accept the repudiation, though, he can immediately cancel the contract, institute suit for breach of contract, and negotiate another agreement with someone else. In his breach of contract suit, the plaintiff must prove that he was ready, willing and able to perform his end of the bargain.

Under the UCC, if one of the parties reasonably believes that the other will not perform according to the terms of the contract, he can suspend performance and ask the other party for assurances that he will perform. In this way, the UCC allows each party to suspend performance without being considered in breach. For example, if the buyer falls behind in his payments, the seller can suspend future deliveries and ask the buyer for some tangible assurance that he won't default. The buyer could, for example, offer a security interest in his property. Under the UCC, if no assurance is given within thirty days, the buyer will be considered in breach.

Installment Contracts

An installment contract is one that calls for multiple deliveries of the goods. A typical installment contract may involve delivery of heating oil in the winter, or the delivery of individual parts for the assembly of a large machine. If the goods in one installment are defective, but the seller assures the buyer that he will cure the defect, the buyer must continue to accept installments and sue (or settle) for any damages caused by the defective installment. Defective goods in one installment do not give the buyer the right to reject the whole contract unless the defect in that one installment substantially impairs the value of the entire lot and the defect cannot be cured. This might occur if one of the delivered machine parts is defective, thereby preventing further assembly of the machine.

Torts

Negligence

The most obvious way for a plaintiff in a tort action to prove that the defendant failed to perform his duty is to present direct evidence about the defendant's actions. Sometimes there is no direct evidence—no witnesses, no written evidence, and no admission by the defendant. When this happens in negligence cases, the law permits the jury—under a doctrine called *res ipsa loquitor* ("the thing speaks for itself")—to infer what happened from circumstantial evidence. To prove negligence under *res ipsa loquitor*, the plaintiff must show that his type of injury does not ordinarily occur in the absence of negligence, and that the defendant's actions were the most likely cause. This doctrine shifts the burden of disproving negligence onto the defendant, who is usually the one best able to tell what actually happened. Suppose, for example, a patient undergoing surgery for an infected gallbladder awakens from anesthesia with nerve damage in one arm. In the lawsuit he can invoke the doctrine of *res ipsa loquitur* ("the thing speaks for itself") to prove negligence. This forces the defendant anesthesiologist to explain what happened when the patient was anesthetized.

Negligence Per Se

Since violations of criminal statutes require a higher burden of proof than violations of civil statutes, it seems obvious that anyone violating a criminal statute must have also violated the corresponding civil law prohibiting negligence. The tricky part is proving that the plaintiff in the civil action was one of the people the criminal statute was trying to protect, and that the plaintiff's injury was exactly the kind of injury the statute was trying to prevent. It may be illegal for a pharmacist to sell outdated drugs, but negligence per se would not apply if the plaintiff died of a disease that would not have been cured by fresh medication.

Was the Defendant's Failure to Perform Excusable?

If the judge finds that the plaintiff and defendant owed each other a duty to perform, and that the defendant did fail to perform, issue number three comes into play: Is the defendant's non-performance excusable? The defense of a lawsuit, of course, does not begin here. Defenses run a wide gamut, beginning with a denial that the plaintiff has standing to sue, and then denying that he (the defendant) failed to perform his legal duty. Only after these defenses fail would a defendant ask the court to excuse his non-performance.

Failure to perform is excused by the courts if one of the following is true: (a) the defendant cannot be sued; (b) the defendant had a good excuse for not performing; (c) the plaintiff was himself in the wrong; or (d) the law permitting suit was unconstitutional or wrong by today's standards.

The Defendant Cannot Be Sued

Privilege and Immunity

The law will excuse non-performance if the defendant is someone society wants to protect from suit, which it does by making them "privileged" or "immune" from suit. Privileged means that the law doesn't even recognize the defendant's bad act as something punishable—such as killing the enemy during wartime, killing in self-defense, and acts by the President for the benefit of the country.

Privilege permits anyone to use reasonable force to protect himself or someone else against physical attack. One may also use reasonable non-deadly force to defend or recapture one's personal property, as long as reasonable attempts are first made to avoid force. A jury may find that a punch in the face was reasonable under the circumstances, but not warning shots from a shotgun. Merchants are given the privilege of reasonably detaining someone suspected of stealing merchandise. A security agent can stop a suspected shoplifter—but performing a strip-search in a private office goes beyond the privilege. Private citizens are priviliged to make warrantless arrests of anyone witnessed committing a misdemeanor, or of anyone they reasonably believe to have committed a felony.

Immunity excuses non-performance in order to achieve a more important social goal. Employers are immune from negligence suits under tort law if the injured employee is already covered by worker's compensation, thus protecting the employer from excessive exposure to liability. Until relatively recently, charitable organizations were immune from tort suits. In the interests of family unity, tort law prohibits a child from suing his parents, and in some states prohibits one spouse from suing another. The government is also immune from tort suits. Only since World War II has the federal government permitted itself to be sued, and only for causes of action listed in the Federal Torts Claims Act.

Statute of Limitations

Probably the most important protector of non-performance is the statute of limitations, which prohibits suits concerning events that have become stale. The law says that after a reasonable period defendants should be freed from the threat of litigation. If, however, the defendant fraudulently prevented the plaintiff from realizing he had a cause of action against the defendant, the statute of limitations would be extended. (Under equity law, losing the right to sue for waiting too long is called "laches.")

Valid Excuses for Non-Performance

The law excuses a defendant's non-performance if the defendant failed to perform due to lack of notice, out of necessity or ignorance, or if performance was impossible or pointless.

Lack of Notice

It is important to keep careful track of dates and exactly who knew what on those dates. The law is very concerned with whether a party was on notice of some critical fact. Lack of notice will often excuse non-performance. But notice is a slippery concept: there is *subjective* notice—the person was actually informed of some fact—and *objective* notice—what any reasonable person under the circumstances would have or should have known; *constructive* notice is public notice that anyone could have learned about by reading public announcements— what he "could have" known; *imputed* notice is what someone under his control actually knew.

Necessity

Emergencies excuse a wide range of non-performance. When an emergency excuses a trespass, the trespasser must pay for any damages (unless the damage was done for the public good, in which case he is protected by privilege). Say, for example, that during a storm a ship captain ties his boat to a nearby pier but the boat pulls away from the pier, damaging the pilings. The ship owner is liable. Suppose during the same storm the city engineer decides to remove dikes from a farmer's land in order to prevent the city from being flooded. The engineer should be protected by privilege.

Impossibility

Impossibility is another frequently raised excuse for non-performance. What's impossible for one person, of course, may be only difficult for another. To be legally impossible, a contract must be objectively impossible to perform—not just more expensive—and the event making performance impossible must have been unforeseen by the defendant and unattributable to some negligent or intentional act by the defendant. For example, land taken over by eminent domain may make it impossible for the landowner to perform a legal duty. Actual or constructive eviction of a tenant relieves him of the duty to pay rent. (Constructive eviction is an act—or failure to act—by the landlord or anyone under the landlord's control that interferes with the tenant's use and enjoyment of the property—e.g., failure to provide adequate hot water, or failure to control a neighbor's noise.)

Death will ordinarily not render a contract void by way of impossibility, unless the contract was for services so unique that only that person could perform its terms.

Illegality

A contract requiring performance of an illegal act (e.g., gambling) will usually amount to impossibility, rendering the contract void.

Destruction of the Subject Matter

Destruction of the subject matter of the contract will also excuse non-performance, but only if the thing destroyed was so unique that substitution is out of the question, as with an antique lamp or a particular plot of land. The UCC imposes an extra duty on the non-performing seller claiming impossibility: the seller must notify the buyer within a reasonable time of the impossibility.

Futility

The law will not make a person do something futile. This principle stems from a famous 1902 case. Henry had contracted to rent a room from Krell from which to view the coronation parade of King Edward VII. The King had a sudden attack of appendicitis and the coronation was cancelled. Krell tried to force Henry to pay for the room anyway. The court declined to force payment reasoning that the performance of the contract was to view the coronation (not just to rent the room):

when the purpose of a contract is frustrated by unforeseen events over which there was no control, and those events make the contract worthless to one party, that party can rescind. The key word here is worthless—not almost worthless, but totally worthless. (Under the UCC, frustration of purpose is called "impracticability.")

Mistake

Mistakes and misunderstandings are used primarily in contract law to deny that a duty was owed or to excuse non-performance. Understandably, the mistake must be about a fundamental aspect of the agreement resulting in a material impact on the duties owed. There are two types of mistakes: "unilateral" (made by one party) and "mutual" (made by both parties). For example, the sale of "costume jewelry" which the purchaser recognizes as real diamonds involves a unilateral mistake. There would be a mutual mistake if both parties thought the gemstones were costume jewelry.

Only the person adversely affected by a mutual mistake can void the contract, and only if he can prove that he did not assume the risk of a mutual mistake. Thus, the seller of costume jewelry would not be able to rescind the contract, because he assumed the risk of inadvertently selling valuable jewelry. With unilateral mistakes the adversely affected party can void the contract only if the party benefitting from the mistake knew or should have known about it, or if enforcing the contract would be unconscionable. This prevents an offeree from snapping up a misquoted "bargain."

Certain Actions by the Plaintiff

Consent

Obviously, a plaintiff who consented to the defendant's failure to perform can hardly complain about it afterwards. The defendant, however, must prove that the plaintiff expressly (through words) or implicitly (through acts) consented, that the plaintiff had both the authority and the freedom to consent, that he had the necessary knowledge to make an informed decision, and that the scope of consent included non-performance of his duty.

Waiver

Under contract law, when one party "waives" non-performance by the other, he agrees to temporarily modify the terms of the contract. A waiver is like an offer, in that the plaintiff is free to revoke his waiver as long as the defendant has not paid consideration for it (which would render the waiver a permanent modification), or detrimentally relied on the waiver.

Suppose, for example, a mortgagor decides to make his mortgage payment two weeks late, and the bank accepts it without complaint. (The person taking out the mortgage is the mortgagor; the bank is the mortgagee.) The mortgagor then pays late for the next few months, and again no complaint. By accepting those late payments, the bank waived the requirement to pay on time. To reestablish its right to demand timely payments, the bank must notify the mortgagor that from now on it is requiring mortgage payments be paid on time. The mortgagor can try to defeat this demand by estoppel, claiming that he has already detrimentally relied on the extra two weeks to pay his mortgage. However, because estoppel is only an equitable (fairness) argument, the defendant will have to convince the court that his new cash flow pattern is fixed and it would now be a serious hardship on him to pay on time.

Assumption-of-Risk

Assumption-of-risk is used as a defense when the plaintiff knowingly exposed himself to the possibility that the defendant would not perform. As a defense to a breach-of-contract suit, assumption-of-risk asserts that the plaintiff knowingly assumed the risk that the defendant might not perform the terms of the contract. Understandably, assumption-of-risk is a difficult defense to sustain in the face of a contract in which each party's obligations are outlined.

In torts, the defendant cannot raise assumption-of-risk as a defense to his negligent act because the law does not allow one to assume the risk of another's negligence. Thus, if a parent accompanies his child on a carousel and is injured as a result of negligently maintained machinery, the owner of the carousel cannot claim that the parent assumed the risk.

Contributory Negligence

In many jurisdictions, contributory negligence by the plaintiff will deny the plaintiff any recovery in a torts claim. To soften that principle, courts utilize the doctrine of "last clear chance": even though the plaintiff was contributorily negligent, the defendant is still liable if the defendant saw the plaintiff in jeopardy, knew the plaintiff did not perceive his jeopardy, and failed to prevent injury to the plaintiff when he could have done so without extraordinary effort. For example: a pedestrian steps off a sidewalk to cross the street against the light; a driver who sees the pedestrian in his path must make every reasonable effort to avoid hitting him. The driver in this case has the last clear chance to avoid an accident. Most jurisdictions now reduce the plaintiff's award by a percentage representing the plaintiff's negligence—called "comparative negligence."

Contributory negligence is no defense to a strict-liabilty claim, but assumption-of-risk is (so long as the plaintiff knew of the danger involved and proceeded unreasonably). Thus, the owner of a wild animal that attacks a negligent trespasser cannot raise the plaintiff's own negligence as a defense. (The defendant's best argument would be that the trespasser knew of the wild animal and knowingly trespassed anyway.)

Fraud

Understandably, the law excuses the defendant's non-performance if the plaintiff dealt with him fraudulently. Fraud is the intentional misrepresentation of a material fact, done with the intent to deceive, and which actually and reasonably does deceive the innocent party.

Each element must be proved: intention to deceive, misrepresentation of a material fact, and actual deception of a reasonable person. If a seller intentionally misrepresents to a buyer that a tractor can safely plow on a 30-degree incline, but the buyer is not deceived, the buyer cannot later claim fraud.

Unclean Hands

In equity, the plaintiff cannot come to the court with "unclean hands." That is, he cannot expect support of his fairness argument if he himself has been underhanded in some way. Someone seeking payment for work not covered by a formal contract may lose his equity argument if the court learns that while on the job he was engaged in drug-dealing.

Some excuses for non-performance are called "affirmative defenses," which place the burden of proof on the defendant. Whether a particular defense is considered an affirmative defense by the court depends on state law. For example, if the defendant claims that he signed a contract under duress, some states require the plaintiff to prove that the defendant was *not* under duress. On the other hand, if the defendant bases his defense on accord and satisfaction, *he* has the burden of proving that he satisfied the accord. Two other common affirmative defenses are assumption of risk and contributory negligence.

Invalid Law

The Constitution is the supreme law of the land and no federal or state law can violate it. In other words, the Constitution imposes a duty on state and federal governments to act in accordance with the Constitution. Failure to do so prevents a state from accusing someone of breaking the law because the law itself is invalid. When two parties define their legal obligations to one another via a contract, the Constitution is generally inapplicable because the Constitution limits governments, not private parties.

There are three major ways to prove a statute unconstitutional: it is void-for-vagueness, overly broad, or in direct violation of the Constitution. Void-for-vagueness means the statute is so vague that one can never be sure when he is violating it. A vague criminal statute is doubly bad because it gives the police unbridled discretion in deciding who has, and who has not, broken the law. Example: "It shall be illegal for suspicious people to loiter in this town." Use of the term "suspicious" gives the police too much leeway to stop whomever they want.

Overbreadth is a doctrine prohibiting the government from passing laws which inadvertently prohibit the exercise of fundamental liberties guaranteed by the Constitution, like free speech, free exercise of religion, raising a family, interstate travel, and voting. These fundamental liberties are so cherished that if a statute makes people even so much as fearful of exercising a fundamental liberty, the law will be struck down as having an unconstitutionally "chilling" effect on one of the fundamental rights. For example, a law that prohibits driving on Sunday may be struck down because it prevents citizens from going to church.

Any law which violates a clause in the Constitution must yield to the Constitution. The most easily offended provisions are the Equal Protection Clause, the Commerce Clause, the Privileges and Immunities Clause, and the Contracts Clause.

The Equal Protection Clause says that a legislature must have a "compelling" reason in singling out a particular religious, racial, or ethnic group for punishment. For example, unless it could be shown that the state has a compelling interest to prohibit a certain class of people from buying more than one case of beer at a time, a statute seeking to do so would be struck down as unconstitutional.

The Commerce Clause serves to maximize interstate commerce. Unless a state has a good reason for burdening interstate commerce, the federal courts will strike down a state law that does so. Thus, a state cannot place a tax on goods shipped from another jurisdiction in order to protect its local industries, but it can limit interstate traffic that poses a serious health hazard to its citizens.

The Privileges and Immunities Clause prohibits states from discriminating against non-residents simply to protect its own citizens. Such discrimination might take the form of a higher income tax on newcomers to a state.

The Contracts Clause prohibits the government from stepping between the parties to a signed contract and changing their contractual obligations.

Besides requiring state laws to obey the Constitution, legislative pecking order also demands that state laws yield to Congressional laws, called the Preemption Doctrine. The most troublesome cases occur when Congress has not yet passed a law regarding the particular issue in question. The courts must then decide whether Congress, by failing to pass legislation, wanted the field left free of all regulation (including that by the states).

Instead of attacking the constitutionality of a statute, the defendant can argue that because of changed technology and new social values, now is the time for the judges to change the law, or at least their interpretation of it. For example, laws prohibiting homosexuality, marijuana use, or driving over 55 mph are all subject to the argument that they are antiquated and should be reinterpreted or overturned.

5

Did the Defendant's Breach Cause the Plaintiff's Injury?

As we have seen, non-performance of a legal duty without an excuse is called a breach, and the plaintiff is entitled to damages for injuries suffered as a result. The key phrase is "as a result of," because the plaintiff must prove that it was the defendant's unexcused failure to perform that caused the injury. Causation is a term of art comprising two elements: the plaintiff must prove that the defendant's actions were the actual cause of his injuries (called cause-in-fact), and that the plaintiff's injuries were foreseeable by the defendant when the defendant was committing the breach (called proximate causation). Cause-in-fact and proximate causation must both be satisfied to prove causation.

Cause-In-Fact

Cause-in-fact means that if it weren't for the defendant's breach of duty, the plaintiff's injury never would have happened. Thus, even when the defendant's act combined with that of another to cause the injury, the defendant will still be liable as long as his act was significant enough that without it, the injury would not have occurred. When the injury results from the combined acts of the defendant and another person—either of whose act alone could have caused the injury—

then both are held "jointly and severably" liable for the injury. ("Jointly" liable means that each defedant is responsible for the entire amount of the plaintiff's damages. "Severally" means that the plaintiff can sue each defendant individually for the full amount. If, for example, the plaintiff recovers 25% from the first defendant, he can then sue the second defendant for the remaining 75%. If the defendants were jointly but not severally liable, the plaintiff would be allowed only one chance to recover; he would have to join both defendants in the same lawsuit.) If the plaintiff's injury resulted from only one act, but the court cannot determine whether it was by the defendant or someone else (either of whom alone could have caused the injury), then both are held jointly and severally liable. If the plaintiff suffered more than one injury at the hands of more than one defendant, and the court can determine which defendant caused which injury, then each will be held responsible only for the injury he caused, even though the defendants' acts may have combined in some way to cause the accident.

Proximate Cause

Proximate cause means that both the plaintiff and the general nature of his injury were foreseeable—either by the defendant or by a reasonable person. In a contract case, the plaintiff is always foreseeable because he is one of the parties. In a tort, whether the plaintiff was foreseeable is a question for the jury—as is whether the plaintiff's injury was the type actually or reasonably anticipated by the defendant. For example, if a plaintiff injures his neck in a car accident and the ambulance driver negligently drops him from the stretcher (fracturing his arm and further aggravating his neck), only the ambulance company will be liable for the fractured arm because being dropped from a stretcher was not foreseeable at the time of the auto accident. Both parties, of course, will be responsible for the neck injuries.

Defenses

There are two defenses to cause-in-fact. The first is that the plaintiff's injuries were going to occur anyway, even without the defendant's breach. This is known as the "but for" or "sine qua non" rule, or the inevitability doctrine.

The second (and more common) defense is that the defendant's breach was not the cause of the plaintiff's injury. The defendant can show this in three ways. First, he can try to refute the plaintiff's direct and circumstantial evidence of causation. Direct evidence are witnesses, writings, and admissions—anything indicating that the defendant's negligence caused the plaintiff's injury. Circumstantial evidence are unspoken and unwritten facts which *imply* that the defendant's negligence caused the plaintiff's injury.

Second, the defendant can try to show that his breach was only one of many possible causes, one of which or all of which were more likely than the defendant's breach to have caused the plaintiff's injury:

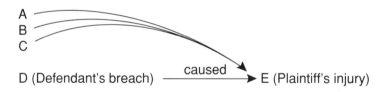

Under some circumstances, the defendant might admit that his breach *would* have caused the plaintiff's injuries, but an unforeseeable event supervened to become the actual cause of the plaintiff's injury. To be relieved of responsibility for the plaintiff's injury, however, the defendant must prove that the supervening event completely replaced (not merely combined with) his own breach as the cause of the plaintiff's injury.

Finally, the defendant can show that the plaintiff's injury was not what one would normally expect as a result of the defendant's breach. The most likely consequence of the breach was not E (plaintiff's injury), but rather F, G, or H:

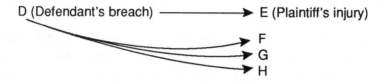

The defense to proximate cause is that either the plaintiff or his injuries were unforeseeable. For example, the plaintiff may not have been in the "zone of danger" at the time of the defendant's negligent act, or some other event supervened to cause unforeseeable injuries.

Pansy is waiting for a traffic light to turn when she is rear-ended by Headlong. Pansy consults her doctor, complaining of persistent headaches. A CAT scan is performed revealing an incidental abnormality unrelated to the headache. During surgery to correct the abnormality, Pansy dies. Her survivors sue Headlong for her death, claiming that Pansy would still be alive were it not for Headlong's negligent act. Here, the defense would successfully argue that the supervening events leading up to Pansy's death were unforeseeable.

This general paradigm applies in any situation in which one is trying to prove that A caused B. Take a criminal case: in front of numerous eyewitnesses, the defendant Bill killed his girlfriend Sally in the restaurant where she worked. To convict Bill of first degree murder, the prosecution must prove that when Bill killed Sally, he did so with intent (i.e., the killing was not accidental), and that Bill formed the intent to kill her *before* entering the restaurant. In other words, if "A" represents the fact that Bill had a motive for killing Sally, and "B" represents the fact that Bill killed Sally with the intent to do so, the prosecution must prove that "A" *caused* "B."

$$ \underset{\text{(Motive)}}{A} \xrightarrow{\text{caused}} \underset{\text{(Intent)}}{B} $$

The defense will first try to prove that A and B did not happen: that Bill never had a motive to kill Sally, and that he killed her accidentally. If, however, the prosecution prevails on both issues—that Bill had a motive to murder and did intentionally kill her, then in order to prove first degree murder, the prosecution must still prove causation: that Bill went to the restaurant with the intent of killing Sally. The prosecution will do this with direct evidence—witnesses who might have heard Bill voice his intent before entering the restaurant, something Bill wrote stating his intent, etc.—and circumstantial evidence from which the jury must infer that Bill went to the restaurant with the intent of killing Sally.

The defense will first try to refute the prosecution's direct evidence by impeaching the prosecution's witnesses and trying to invalidate any writings. The defense will then combat the prosecution's circumstantial evidence by showing that even if A were true (that Bill had a motive to kill Sally), the natural consequence of A would have been C or D, but not B. That is, even if Bill had the motive to kill Sally, he would not have been foolish enough to do so in a busy restaurant where the murder would certainly be witnessed.

Alternatively, the defense will try to prove that even if B were true— that Bill did kill Sally with intent, his intent did not form until after entering the restaurant when they got into an argument. In other words, the cause of B was not A, but a heated agument, E.

Remedies

Legal

Contracts

In general, courts want to put the parties in the positions they would have enjoyed had they both adhered to their contractual obligations. To do this, five questions must be answered:

1) How much money has the plaintiff (the non-breaching party) already spent?

2) How much did he expect to spend to fulfill his end of the bargain?

3) How much money has the plaintiff already received from the defendant?

4) How much more money would he have received had the contract not been breached?

5) How much had the defendant's property increased in value at the time of the breach. (*See bar graph.*)

Without a breach, the plaintiff would have been made a profit: $3 + 4$ less $1 + 2$. The value of such a profit is called "expectancy damages." If, however, the plaintiff knows that he would have had many more expenses than listed in 2—enough that he would have ended up with a loss—plaintiff will instead seek "reliance damages" (his out-of-pocket expenses less what the defendant has already paid him). If it

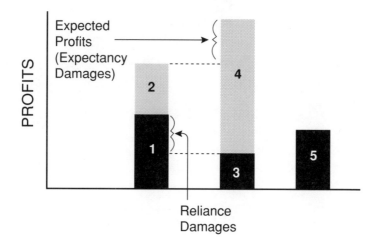

turns out that the defendant's property has already increased in value (5), more than plaintiff's reliance damages (1 less 3), the plaintiff can also seek "restitution damages" (5) under quasi-contract—arguing that the defendant should not be allowed to benefit from his breach.

Under the Uniform Commercial Code, a breach occurs when one of the parties either repudiates the contract or fails to perform. That is, the seller either refuses to deliver the goods or delivers non-conforming goods, or the buyer either wrongfully refuses to accept the goods or accepts them but does not pay for them.

When the buyer is in breach, the seller can either (a) withhold delivery of the goods, (b) sell those goods which he had already made under the contract, or (c) recover damages for those conforming goods he cannot sell; sometimes the seller can recover the contract price of the goods. (UCC 2-703, 2-704, 2-705, 2-706, 2-708, 2-709)

When the seller is in breach, the buyer can (a) "cover" by purchasing substitute goods and recover damages, (b) recover damages for nondelivery, or (c) recover goods already made for the contract;

sometimes the buyer can get specific performance of the contract. (UCC 2-711, 2-712, 2-713, 2-716)

What if the defendant's breach of contract caused a chain reaction? Perhaps a machine was not delivered on time, and as a result production fell behind schedule; buyers got angry; orders were cancelled; profits lost. Should the machine manufacturer have to pay for all these "consequential" damages? The general rule is that the defendant is responsible for any damages caused by his breach so long as that's what the parties agreed to (or would have agreed to had the subject arisen), and so long as the court does not have to guess at the value of the lost profits.

Both parties, of course, would like to avoid being responsible for consequential damages. They can do this by stipulating in the contract what they will be responsible for, or by setting a dollar value—called "liquidated damages"—in case one party breaches.

Torts

Under tort law, the plaintiff can ask the court for monetary damages to compensate him for his past and future damages—including pain and suffering, lost wages, medical expenses, loss of consortium, and (if the plaintiff suffered a physical injury) mental distress.

Equitable

Specific performance and injunctions are equitable solutions granted when an award of monetary damages would be unsatisfactory. For example, if the subject matter of the contract is so unique that money cannot substitute, the court will force the defendant to perform his end of the bargain. The sale of real property is a prime example, because every piece of property is considered unique.

Other examples of equitable solutions include rescission (complete undoing) of a contract, reformation (rewriting) of a contract, accounting (of profits and losses), partition (dividing of property), and contribution (reimbursement from other culpable parties).

Alternative Dispute Resolution

Even where one party has been clearly wronged, his best remedy may not be by way of a lawsuit. America is easily the most litigious country in the world, and its civil courts are clogged to the point that cases are sometimes postponed for months and years. Not only is it time-consuming to bring suit, it can be very expensive as well.

The logic of lawyering does not always dictate going to court. There are numerous extra-judicial remedies available, most of them involving a third-party intermediary. Such solutions are especially appropriate when both sides have good legal arguments to support their positions. The parties may choose to avoid the time and expense of litigation by submitting to conciliation, negotiation, mediation, arbitration, or a combination of those processes—in which lawyers can (though they don't necessarily have to) play the roles of advocates.

Conciliation is simply a sincere attempt by two parties to a dispute to resolve their differences amicably, without resorting to lawyers or courts or mediators. Once the parties vent their grievances face to face, the problem is often resolved quickly and to their mutual satisfaction; adjudication will firmly favor one legal position over another, but it can often leave the parties bitter and unreconciled.

The parties may *negotiate* the terms of a settlement, either directly or through their lawyers. Usually (but not always) negotiation is initiated by the defendant (who has the most to lose in money damages)—particularly if his misconduct has been intentional or clearly negligent. The plaintiff may welcome a fair settlement in order to avoid protracted litigation.

Mediation is the most common form of alternative dispute resolution. It requires an independent mediator acceptable to both parties, who meets with them in a non-adversarial setting and attempts to formulate an agreement between them. The goal is a fairly balanced compromise. The agreement is not binding on either party unless they both agree, at which time the compromise takes the form of a contract.

Arbitration is binding mediation. That is, the parties mutually agree upon an independent arbiter to hear their case and render an opinion binding on both parties. Arbitration clauses are often placed in employment contracts and other commercial agreements, whereby the parties agree in advance that should any dispute arise over terms of the contract it will be resolved by way of arbitration rather than court adjudication.

Newer dispute-resolution processes involve variations or combinations of those mentioned above, such as "med-arb" (if the mediation fails, it will trigger arbitration); "rent-a-judge" (the parties hire a retired jurist to hear the facts and render an advisory opinion); and "mini-trials" or "summary jury trials" (a jury hears the facts and arrives at a non-binding verdict).

Evidence

The five "major" elements for any cause of action are duty, failure to perform, no excuses, causation, and damages. Each major element may be subdivided into single words or phrases. For breach of contract, the major sub-elements of duty are as follows.

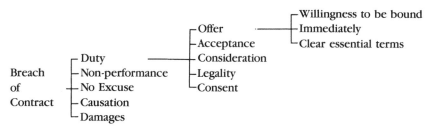

Proving breach of contract means proving each of the terminal words and phrases. Doing that involves explaining what the law means by each word or phrase, presenting the facts in the case, and fitting the legal definition of the terminal word or phrase to the facts. Thus, there are "legal" issues—what is the exact meaning of the law; "factual" issues—what actually happened; and "application" issues—do the facts of this case indicate that the defendant conformed to the law?

Although the terminal words and phrases of a cause of action may seem unambiguous, every word in English is open to varying interpretations. Ultimately, the meaning of the terminal words and phrases is up to the judge. The factual issues, however, are decided by the jury, based on evidence introduced at trial in the form of testimony from witnesses, documents, and tangible objects.

Credibility

To be admissible, all evidence must be both relevant and trustworthy. The judge decides whether evidence is relevant and trustworthy enough to be admitted; the jury decides how trustworthy the admitted evidence actually is.

A judge is not a referee—that is, he doesn't blow a whistle as soon as he sees an infraction of the rules. A judge decides if there is an infraction only if asked to do so. What this means is that untrustworthy testimony may be admitted unless the opposing attorney voices objection and asks the judge for a ruling. Of course, a judge will object on his own when he sees an error so egregious that it jeopardizes a fair trial.

Judges require proof of at least four things before declaring a witness' testimony trustworthy enough to be admitted. First, the witness must have first-hand knowledge of whatever he is testifying about. Second, he must be able to remember that first-hand experience at trial. Third, he must be trustworthy himself. And fourth, he must be able to communicate his thoughts to the jury so that they can understand what he is saying.

A lawyer "impeaches" a witness when he brings out evidence discrediting the witness' trustworthiness, that is, when the witness shows a lack of first-hand knowledge, inadequate memory, untrustworthiness, or an inability to communicate his thoughts.

First-Hand Knowledge

If a witness does not have first-hand knowledge of what he is testifying about, he is no better able than any of the jurors to decide what happened. More important, the jury cannot tell whether the event was accurately witnessed if the person who actually saw the event is not on the witness stand to be cross-examined.

The court makes an exception for "experts," who are permitted to tell the jury what happened without first-hand knowledge because they can reconstruct what happened from the facts given to them. (That's why they're experts.)

If the person with first-hand knowledge is not in court, the judge will sometimes settle for the next best thing: hearsay. Hearsay is what the witness with first-hand knowledge told another person. We ask the other person to take the stand and tell the court what he was told about the event. Judges don't like hearsay for obvious reasons: the person on the stand may be mistaken or lying about what the witness with first-hand knowledge told him, or the testimony may be inaccurate because the witness with first-hand knowledge may have misperceived the event in question. The court would much rather have that witness with first-hand knowledge available for cross-examination.

When it has to, the court will accept hearsay as the truth. Before it does, though, the court wants some assurances that the witness on the stand is trustworthy, and that whatever the witness with first-hand knowledge reported to him is also trustworthy. The types of hearsay which the court will admit as truthful are called the "hearsay exceptions." The list of hearsay exceptions is long, and recognizing hearsay exceptions amidst the give and take of courtroom testimony is one reason experienced trial attorneys earn their fee.

Memory

If a witness can't remember what he saw or heard at the time of the event in question, there's no point in his taking the stand. And if he forgets while on the stand, there's no point in continuing unless the attorney can jog his memory. The court will allow the attorney to jog a forgetful witness' memory, so long as the attorney is not simply feeding the witness answers.

Another way around a lapsed memory is to introduce a statement made by the testifying witness soon after he observed the event. The witness need only vouch for the fact that when he made the statement, the event was fresh in his mind.

Lying

About the only time a court will declare a witness so deceitful that he cannot be allowed to testify is if the witness is a convicted perjurer. Once he testifies, however, the jury decides how truthful he is. Opposing attorneys may try to show that a witness is likely to lie because he is biased, because he has lied under oath in the past, because he committed a crime involving misrepresentation (e.g., theft), or because he has a reputation in the community for lying. Evidence that the witness told someone else a different story also makes the witness' testimony untrustworthy because the jury doesn't know which story to believe.

Communication

If the witness's thoughts can't be understood or translated into English, he is removed from the stand. Simple as that.

Relevancy

Just because a document or a witness' statement is trustworthy does not mean the jury should hear everything he has to say. The testimony must also satisfy the other requirement for admissibility: relevancy. (A related concept is materiality. A statement is material if it helps prove a point; that point, however, may not be relevant to the issue in dispute.)

Logical Relevancy

If the four rules of trustworthiness are a check on the witness, relevancy is a check on the attorney. In a trial, when an attorney wants to introduce a piece of evidence, opposing counsel must ask two questions. First, is the evidence authentic? If not, it should be discarded as irrelevant. Second, if the evidence *is* what the attorney purports it to be, will it really help the jury decide the issue in dispute? If it won't, the evidence is likewise irrelevant and therefore inadmissible.

Suppose the attorney tries to introduce a gun into evidence, claiming it belongs to the defendant. If witnesses can't convince the jury that this is the defendant's gun, it becomes irrelevant. Even if it is the defendant's gun, it is irrelevant if the victim was knifed to death.

Questions of authenticity arise all the time. Lazy Susan is contesting her Uncle Bigbuck's will. Her attorney presents another will to the court in which Uncle Bigbuck left his entire estate to Lazy Susan. Unless the attorney can show that the signature at the bottom is Uncle Bigbuck's, this second will is deemed irrelevant.

Suppose that in a criminal trial, the state's attorney introduces a bag of powder and claims that it contains the heroin found in the defendant's apartment. To prove it, he will have to put on the stand the arresting officer and any others who had access to the bag; he then must trace the bag of heroin from its discovery in the apartment to the police station evidence locker, to the police analysis lab, back to the police evidence locker, and finally to its arrival in court, demonstrating that this bag is the one found in the defendant's apartment and that no one could have slipped heroin into the bag to frame the defendant.

Legal Relevancy

Logically relevant evidence may still be inadmissible if it jeopardizes a fair trial. Stated another way, evidence can be logically relevant but not legally relevant. This happens when the evidence has such an emotional taint to it that the jury will disregard the logic of the evidence and vote their emotional reaction. The judge must weigh how much the logic of the evidence will help the jury arrive at the truth against how much the emotionality of the evidence will misdirect the jury away from the truth. If the judge finds the evidence too prejudicial to a fair trial, he will exclude it.

Rules and Inferences

Best Evidence Rule

Written documents pose special evidentiary problems. If the court wants to examine the *contents* of a writing, a copy won't do because there is too much chance it could be altered. This duty to produce the original document when the contents of the writing are at issue is called the "Best Evidence Rule," and applies to writings and photographs. Like all duties, failure to produce the original may be excused—for example, if the original was lost or destroyed, or is in the hands of the opposing party who won't surrender it.

Original writings may still be inadmissible if their contents include hearsay. Therefore all writings (including contracts) must satisfy three evidentiary rules: relevancy (authenticity and logical and legal relevancy), the best evidence rule, and the rule against hearsay.

Contradicting the Terms of a Contract: Parol Evidence Rule

It's tough for a party to argue that the contract admitted into evidence is not what he agreed to. It's doubly difficult when he wants to introduce oral evidence to contradict the written terms. The "Parol Evidence Rule" specifically prohibits oral testimony that contradicts the written terms of a contract. After all, the court does not want to hear one party claiming "He said this," and the other party claiming "No, I didn't," when there exists a written statement of their agreement. The court sometimes disregards the Parol Evidence Rule if the person denying the contract is a consumer, because it recognizes that few consumers read what they sign. But businessmen (or their lawyers) *are* expected to read and understand what they sign.

One way to contradict the terms of a contract with oral testimony is to convince the court that the term got into the agreement through fraud or mistake. Oral testimony is also admissible to contradict a specific term of the contract if the term is ambiguous or was intended to deal with an entirely separate matter.

Inferences

Often a jury doesn't have all the facts it would like. Under some circumstances, the judge will allow the jury to infer a fact from testimony introduced at trial. For example, if the plaintiff testifies that he mailed the defendant a properly addressed letter, the judge may allow the jury to infer that the defendant received it. There are different grades of inferences. One is called a *prima facie* case. If the plaintiff presents uncontroverted evidence, and the judge tells the jury that the plaintiff has presented a prima facie case, the jury is free to believe or not believe that the defendant received the letter. If the judge tells the jury that the plaintiff has presented a *presumptive* case, then the jury must believe that the defendant received the letter until the defendant presents trustworthy evidence that he did not receive the letter. In some states, when the defendant presents evidence rebutting the presumption, the jury can no longer presume anything about the properly mailed letter; the plaintiff has to present his own evidence that the defendant received it. In other states, when the defendant presents evidence rebutting the presumption, it still stands, and the jury simply weighs the defendant's evidence against the presumption.

Privilege

Privilege extends into the rules of evidence to protect defendants from adverse testimony. For example, in a criminal trial a person cannot be forced to testify against his or her spouse. In a similar vein, a defendant in a criminal case can (on the basis of privilege) block the state from introducing into evidence any private conversations he might have had with his spouse during their marriage—or with his attorney, priest, psychiatrist, or (in most states) doctor.

Summary

Cases go to trial because there are issues which the parties cannot resolve themselves. In Chapter 9 you will find actual cases (as taken from bar examinations) which raise common legal issues. The issues raised—like those of almost any legal case—can quickly be identified by sytematically walking through the now familiar steps of logic delineated in the first seven chapters.

1. Did the defendant owe the plaintiff a duty to perform? [Chapter 2]

   a. What branch of the law says a legal relationship existed between the plaintiff and defendant? Within that branch of the law, does common law, statutory law, equity, or all three apply?

	Common Law	Statutory Law	Equity
Contracts			
Torts			
Real Property			
Constitutional Law			
Professional Ethics			

b. What was the nature of the relationship?

— CONTRACTS —

Common Law	Statutory Law	Equity
Contractual parties	UCC	One who detrimentally
Third party beneficiary	Warranty:	relied on the defend-
Suretor/Guarantor	foreseeable user	ant's promise or actions
Fiduciary	manufacturer	
Employment	assembler	
employee	distributor	
independent	seller	
contractor	Corporation	
Agency	Worker's Compensation	
principal–agent	Bankruptcy	
Partnership		
general partner		
limited partner		

— TORTS —

Common Law	Statutory Law	Equity
Foreseeable plaintiff		
negligence		
strict liability		
product liability		
Joint tortfeasors		
Landowner		
business invitee		
social guest		
licensee		
trespasser		

— REAL PROPERTY—

Common Law	Statutory Law	Equity
Joint tenants		
Tenants in common		
Tenants by the entirety		
Landlord–tenant		
Buyer–seller		
Easement holder—		
owner of servient		
estate		
Licensor–licensee		
Covenant holder—		
promisor (or		
successor)		

— CONSTITUTIONAL LAW —

Common Law	Statutory Law	Equity
	Equal Protection Clause	
	Commerce Clause	
	Privileges and	
	Immunities Clause	
	Contracts Clause	
	Taking Clause (Fifth	
	Amendment)	

c. Was the relationship valid at the time of the breach?

Under contracts, for example, were all the elements of a contract satisfied?; did the contract fall under the Statute of Frauds?;* did the alleged third party beneficiary rely on the contract before it was changed?; was the defendant employee on the job?; was the agent's status disclosed to the plaintiff?; did the limited partner lose his status by acting like a general partner?; was the sale valid, and if so, which warranty was given?; was the corporation still in existence?

Examples under torts include, was the plaintiff foreseeable?; should strict liability apply?; was the plaintiff's handling of the product foreseeable?; can the injury from each tortfeasor be determined?; did the business invitee, social guest, or licensee become a trespasser before the alleged breach?

Some examples under real property are, did the joint tenancy relationship change before the alleged breach?; was the tenant a subtenant?; was the party an easement holder or a licensee?; did the original promise fulfill all the elements of a covenant?; did the successor in interest need (and fulfill) horizontal and vertical privity in order to sue?

d. What duty was owed by the defendant?

---

* Recall that contracts falling under the Statute of Frauds are protected by the parol evidence rule and the best evidence rule. Contracts can be "removed" from the Statute of Frauds (so no writing will be necessary to prove a contract) by applying the law of equity—substantial performance, unequivocal reference, estoppel, and quasi-contract; by the defendant's admission; or under the UCC, acceptance of payment for goods that are unique, or when there is an "unanswered memo."

2. Did the defendant fail to perform? [Chapter 3]

— CONTRACTS —

<u>Common Law</u>	<u>Statutory Law</u>	<u>Equity</u>
Accord and satisfaction		
Part performance		
Anticipatory breach		

— TORTS —

<u>Common Law</u>	<u>Statutory Law</u>	<u>Equity</u>
Negligence per se		
Res ipsa loquitor		

3. Was the defendant's failure to perform excusable? [Chapter 4]

   a. The defendant cannot be sued because of:
- Lack of standing
- Privilege
- Immunity
- Statute of limitations

   b. The defendant had a good excuse because of:
- Lack of notice
- Necessity
- Impossibility
- Duress
- Illegality
- Destruction of the subject matter
- Futility
- Mistake
- Incapacity

   c. The plaintiff should not be allowed to sue because he:
- Consented
- Waived or ratified
- Assumed the risk
- Was contributorily negligent
- Committed fraud
- Had unclean hands

    d.   The law requiring a duty is unenforceable because it was:
           Pre-empted by the federal Constitution
           Unconstitutional (void for vagueness, overbreadth)
           Out of date, archaic

4. Did the defendant's breach cause the plaintiff's injury?
    [Chapter 5]

    a.   Cause-in-fact (actual) injury

    b.   Foreseeable injury

    What are the plaintiff's damages?

5. What remedies are available? [Chapter 6]

    a.   Legal
           Monetary damages

    b.   Equitable
           Rescission of contract
           Reformation of contract
           Specific performance
           Injunction
           Accounting
           Partition
           Contribution

    c.   Alternative dispute resolution

6. Are all the issues provable in court? [Chapter 7]

    a.   Evidentiary problems
           Relevancy
              Logical
              Legal
           Trustworthiness
           Best evidence rule
           Parol evidence rule
           Inferences
           Privilege

    b.   Civil procedure problems

9

Practice Cases

Lee v. Grant

Lee and Grant owned adjoining tracts of land in Howard County, Maryland. The property line was the center of a 12-foot-wide vacant strip which ran between their respective homes. Lee owned another tract (Green Acre) containing 60 acres which adjoined the rear boundaries of both Lee's and Grant's property, and to which the 12-foot strip extended. Lee's 60-acre tract was unimproved and Grant wanted to buy it to start an apple orchard and to use the 12-foot strip for access to Green Acre. There was no other reasonably available access to the tract. Lee only rarely used the 12-foot strip to gain access to Green Acre. Lee sold the 60-acre tract to Grant but refused to sell his half of the 12-foot strip. He did, however, orally agree to permit Grant to use his half of it in connection with his orchard operation. Grant paved the entire strip and has for five years used it for access to his orchard.

Last summer, Lee picked several baskets of fruit from trees on Grant's property which overhung his land. Grant demanded payment for the apples and Lee refused. In retaliation, Lee cut off the over-hanging branches and roots that extended onto his land. He then erected on his property and within and along the 12-foot strip a high fence which prohibited Grant from using the full width of the strip for his trucks. It also obstructed the light and air to the first floor of Grant's house.

Discussion

The applicable law is real property law. The legal relationship between the parties depends on whether property law defines the strip as an easement or a license. Grant used the strip for five years, which he could only have done if he had a *right* to use the strip (because it was an easement) or *permission* to use the strip (because he had a license). If Grant is considered an easement holder, then Lee owes Grant a duty to allow him to use the 12-foot strip. Lee's building of the fence would be considered a breach of that duty, and he would therefore have to take down the fence and allow Grant continued use of the easement. If Grant's use of the strip is a license, however, Lee's duty to Grant would last only as long as Lee wanted it to; by revoking Grant's license, Lee could cancel any duty he owed Lee, and could therefore keep the fence.

Grant cannot claim that the strip was an easement by express grant because Lee refused to sell his half of the strip, but he can claim that the strip was an implied easement. Easements by implication occur when the dominant and servient estates were once held in common ownership, the owner of the servient estate knew or should have known that the parcel of land in question was being used on a regular basis as if it were an easement, and that continued use of the parcel in question is reasonably necessary to the enjoyment of the dominant estate.

In this case, the 60-acre tract and Lee's property were once owned by Lee, Lee used the 12-foot strip as an easement to get to the 60-acre tract, and as there was no other reasonably available access to the tract, the 12-foot-wide strip is reasonably necessary to its enjoyment.

Grant can also claim that the strip was an easement by necessity since the tract and the strip were once owned by Lee at the time of the sale, and there was no other access except by the strip. Lee can counter that Grant's half of the strip provides sufficient access to the tract, making Lee's half unnecessary.

Grant cannot claim easement by prescription because he has not used the strip for the requisite 20 years.

The fact that Grant spent considerable money to pave the strip undercuts Lee's argument that Grant had only a revocable license to use the strip.

If, as is likely, the court finds that Grant owned an easement, Grant will ask for specific performance, namely, removing the fence and allowing Grant continued use of the easement.

The issue of the fruit is governed by tort law, under which Lee owed Grant a duty to return Grant's property because Lee knew that Grant owned the fruit and had not abandoned it. Thus, when Lee picked fruit from Grant's tree, his unexcused failure to return the fruit breached that duty, constituting the tort of conversion. Grant will ask for monetary damages equaling the value of the fruit (minus the cost of harvesting and marketing the fruit).

As for the overhanging branches and roots—governed by real property law—Grant owed Lee a duty to keep them off Lee's property because each owner owns the air space above and the ground below his property line. Failure to do so without sufficient justification constitutes a trespass, giving Lee the right to use reasonable means to remove the branches and roots. "Reasonable means" means that Lee is liable for the death of any trees resulting from his cutting the roots.

Grant will only prevail in a suit to enforce a "negative easement" of light and air if he can show that Lee's fence was so high that it unreasonably restricted light and air from reaching Grant's property.

Wan v. Wan

In 1983, Don Wan deserted his wife, Iris, leaving her in possession of the farm which they owned as tenants by the entireties. In June 1985, Iris, believing Don to be dead, conveyed the farm as surviving tenant to Will. In December 1985, Iris received a Christmas card from Don postmarked Paris. She then filed for and obtained a divorce from Don in 1987. She immediately married Sam, and, after a short but happy union, died in 1990, devising all of her real and personal property to Sam. Don, Will, and Sam each claim an interest in the farm.

Discussion

This case is governed by real property law, the common law of estates and trusts, and equity law. Don and Iris owned the farm as tenants by the entirety, imposing a duty on Iris not to convey the farm without Don's permission. Iris's mistaken belief that Don was dead when she sold the farm to Will in 1985 had no effect on Don's rightful claim to half the farm.

The divorce in 1987 converted Don and Iris's relationship from tenants by the entirety to tenants in common. Don retained his half ownership of the farm, but the law of equity—through the doctrine of estoppel by deed—prevents Iris's estate from claiming (correctly) that her sale to Will was illegal, and that the sale should therefore be rescinded. Since she intended to sell the property, it would be unfair to allow her to benefit by her mistake about Don's death. Therefore, Will gets Iris's half of the property and becomes a tenant in common with Don.

Jim v. Bob

Bob was looking for a car to pull his new trailer on a cross country trip. While driving down the street one day he saw a "FOR SALE" sign in the window of a car that was parked at a gas station. Bob pulled in and asked the attendant about the car. The attendant said that Jim, the owner, worked as a cook in the diner down the street. Jim came to the gas station after a telephone call from Bob.

Bob explained to Jim that he wanted a car to pull a trailer. Jim said that the car was a 1988 Ford LTD with plenty of power. After a test drive around the block, Bob decided to buy the car. Bob did not have enough money to pay the full agreed upon $6000 price, so Jim said that Bob could pay $2000 down and the balance in 12 equal monthly installments plus interest. Jim presented Bob with a note to evidence this arrangement which Bob signed.

Two weeks after buying the car Bob hitched his trailer to it to start on his trip. He found out that the car did not have enough power to pull the trailer, a very big deluxe "Supertrailerhome," up the first big hill. When he took the car to a shop to see if the car needed tuning, he learned that the car was a 1986 model that was never powerful enough to pull the trailer.

Bob comes to you and asks for advice. You have determined that a 1986 Ford LTD is worth $2000 less than a 1988 model. Bob wants to get out of the agreement. What advice do you give Bob?

Discussion

I would advise Bob that he can sue under breach of warranty and under breach of statutory law, namely, the Uniform Commercial Code (UCC). Jim expressly warranted that the car was a 1988 Ford LTD with plenty of power, an assertion that formed the basis of the bargain. That Jim was not a merchant is irrelevant for express warranties but it does prevent Bob from suing under a breach of warranty of merchantability.

Jim only knew that Bob wanted a car to pull a trailer, obviously to include pulling it up hills. If the car could not pull even a reasonably sized trailer up hills, then Jim breached his implied warranty for a particular purpose because Jim knew that Bob was relying on his knowledge of the car's capacity to pull trailers. Jim will defend that Bob was unjustified in relying on Jim's knowledge of the car's trailer-towing capability because Jim was only a cook.

Under the UCC, a buyer who accepts goods can revoke his acceptance after a reasonable time if the goods are non-conforming and the defect (which must substantially impair the value of the goods) was not discoverable at the time of acceptance. Bob will have to argue that under the circumstances, two weeks is not too long to revoke acceptance. The UCC also requires Bob to notify Jim of his revocation and to make the car available to Jim to retrieve.

If the court finds in Bob's favor on these issues, Bob will ask for the return of his $2000 down payment. The UCC gives Bob the option of selling the car and buying another car that will tow a heavy trailer, then asking the court to assess Jim the difference. The UCC also allows

Bob to keep the car and simply pay Jim another $2000—what the car is really worth.

Sam v. Union

Sam and Sally Simpson were married in 1985 in Montgomery County, Maryland. Throughout their married life, both Sam and Sally were employed on a full-time basis. Sam was self employed as a welder and Sally was employed as a bindery worker in a book bindery. Sally's position afforded her the opportunity to maintain membership in the local bindery worker's union providing very beneficial health care benefits as well as insurance coverage and other benefits. In January 1990, the bindery union offered its members an opportunity to participate in a legal services plan. The plan offered individual and, for a higher premium, family membership, and provided for a set monthly premium (deducted from the employee's paycheck), legal services for individual members and, if family coverage were elected, for spouses and minor children of members.

The agreement stated specifically that it provides members of the plan with legal representation for the preparation of wills, the handling of traffic cases and divorce matters.

The premium was paid to the union which contracted with a large law firm to handle all legal services under the plan. The law firm was selected by the union because of its acknowledged expertise in criminal, civil, and domestic trial work. Because of the small cost of membership and the belief that both she and her husband should prepare wills, Sally, without consulting Sam, joined the legal services plan, subscribing to the family plan.

Approximately six months after joining the plan, Sam and Sally separated due to Sally's discovery of Sam's infidelity. Sally contracted the legal services plan's law firm to draw up a separation agreement. Sally did not change her benefits package. Within a few weeks, Sam, having learned of Sally's membership in the plan, contacted the union to determine how to obtain legal assistance in his domestic dispute. A union representative advised Sam that the law firm retained under the plan would not represent him, and thus no benefits were available. Sam comes to you for advice as to his entitlement to the legal services specified under the plan. Advise fully.

Discussion

The only way Sam can impose a duty on the union to provide him with legal counsel is to prove that he is a third party beneficiary to Sally's contract with the union. To sue as a third party beneficiary, Sam must show not only that Sally intended the contract to benefit him, but also that he 1) acknowledged and agreed to the contract, 2) relied on the contract, or 3) instituted suit to enforce the contract. The facts support Sam's claim: when Sally chose the family plan she intended the contract to benefit Sam, and Sam has since acknowledged and agreed to the contract.

The law firm chosen by the union to represent Sally cannot also represent Sam, but that does not relieve the union of a duty to provide legal counsel with another law firm.

Al v. Mike

On February 28, 1991, Al Arms and Bob Boyd were bird hunting. They were accompanied by a professional guide, Mike Marker, and his pointer dog. This was the third occasion on which Mike had been a guide for Al and Bob and he knew them both to be experienced hunters.

On February 28, the three men had been hunting for more than an hour and had had some success in their hunting when an accident occurred. They were hunting in an open field where there was underbrush but no visual obstruction. The men were all facing in the same direction; Bob and Mike were not far apart, about 30 yards to the left of Al. The dog was on point in front of the three men and to the left of Mike. A single bird took flight and it headed past Bob and Mike, straight toward Al. Al caught a glimpse of the quail out of the corner of his eye, quickly pivoted to his left and without hesitation shot in the direction of Bob and Mike, even though he was aware that they were within his general line of fire. Pellets from the shell hit both men in the face and Mike was severely injured.

Mike has filed suit against Al. What defense will Al raise and will he be successful? Explain.

Discussion

Mike is suing Al for negligence under tort law. Al's defense is that Mike assumed the risk of being accidentally shot. This argument will prevail only if Al can prove his shot was not negligent. If, as is likely, Mike can prove that Al was negligent for firing in Mike's direction without taking better aim, Al's defense of assumption of risk will fail. Mike did not assume the risk that Mike would act negligently.

Mae v. Rental

Mae has filed suit in the Circuit Court for Prince George's County, Maryland, against Rental, Inc., and Maintenance, Inc. At trial the following facts are proved:

In January of 1991, Mae entered an automatic electric elevator in the office building where she worked and traveled to the eighth floor. As she exited the elevator, it suddenly rose two to three inches causing her to fall and fracture her leg.

The building was owned and managed by Rental, Inc. Rental had contracted with Maintenance, Inc. to keep the elevators in proper repair and good working condition.

The electrical and mechanical controls for the elevator were located in the basement of the building in a room to which the only keys were in the possession of Rental and Maintenance.

One week prior to the accident, an employee of Maintenance had replaced a leveling switch on the elevator ridden by Mae.

Upon proof of the above facts at trial, can Mae recover against Rental or Maintenance or both?

Discussion

As landlord, Rental owes Mae a duty (imposed by real property law) to maintain the common areas, including the elevator. Rental failed to maintain the elevator in proper working order, and that failure caused Mae's fractured leg. If Mae sues Rental, Rental will sue Maintenance for breach of its contract with Rental for failing "to keep the elevators in proper repair and good working condition."

Mae can also sue Rental in torts, claiming that Rental was negligent in maintaining the elevator in proper working order. While the exact act of negligence is unknown, the cause of the injury was faulty control of the elevator. Since the elevator controls were under Rental's control, and their malfunction does not normally occur in the absence of negligence, by res ipsa loquitur, Rental must have been negligent, and that negligence caused Mae's injury. The problem with this analysis is that the elevator controls were not under Rental's exclusive control. The same problem arises if Mae sues Maintenance in torts. Therefore, I would recommend that in addition to suing Rental and Maintenance individually, Mae should sue Rental and Maintenance together as joint tortfeasors.

Mae's suit against Maintenance in torts would aver that Rental had turned over responsibility for the elevators to Maintenance, an independent contractor. Maintenance's defense is that it was not an independent contractor but rather an employee of Rental, and as an employee, the employer (Rental) is ultimately (vicariously) responsible.

Whether Maintenance was an employee or independent contractor will depend primarily on the nature of the work and the degree of control that Rental exercised over Maintenance's work. In this case, technical work like elevator servicing is the type of work normally given to an independent contractor. Discovery will be necessary to learn how much control Rental exercised over Maintenance. The mere fact that the elevator key was accessible to Rental does not necessarily indicate that Rental supervised Maintenance's work. Maintenance will likely be found to be an independent contractor, and therefore responsible to Mae (a foreseeable plaintiff) for its negligent servicing of the elevator.

Arnold v. Zerwitz, et al.

Arnold owns a small commercial building and corner lot in South Baltimore which he leased in 1989 to Bertha by a written lease for ten years, at a rental of $500 per month. Bertha was to maintain the property in good repair. The lease contained a covenant against assignment or sublease without Arnold's consent. After one year had run on the lease, Bertha subleased the property in 1980 to Carter, without discussing it with Arnold, for the same $500 per month, which Carter paid directly to Arnold.

A year later, in November of 1990, Arnold agreed to sell the property to Zerwitz subject to the existing lease. Under the contract between Arnold and Zerwitz the property was to be conveyed on March 1, 1991. In an attempt to save money, Arnold and Zerwitz wrote their own contract which made no mention of insurance on the building or who would bear any risk of loss before settlement. On February 24, while there was no one in the building, an illegal space heater used by Carter in the building tipped over and started a fire. The fire caused extensive damage to the building. The best estimate to restore the building indicates it could be completed by April 15, 1991.

Arnold had carried insurance on the building and was paid $50,000 by his insurance company. Zerwitz had not taken out any insurance on the building. Carter immediately abandoned the building. Bertha notified Arnold that she was terminating the lease effective immediately because of the damage to the building. Arnold wrote to Zerwitz insisting that Zerwitz go through with the contract to buy the property on March 1.

Zerwitz has come to you to seek your advice as to whether or not he can be forced to go through with the contract and what rights, if any, he has against Arnold, Bertha, or Carter if he does purchase the property.

Discussion

Arnold v. Zerwitz

Arnold and Zerwitz have a valid contract imposing a duty on Zerwitz to take title to the building. Zerwitz cannot claim a defense of destruction of the subject matter of the contract because the building was not destroyed, only damaged. Nor can Zerwitz claim futility because the building *can* be repaired.

Since the contract made no mention of insurance on the building or who would bear any risk of loss before settlement, the common law doctrine of equitable conversion would impose a duty on Zerwitz to pay for any damage to the property occurring before Zerwitz took possession. However, any insurance proceeds paid to Arnold for the damage would go to Zerwitz.

Zerwitz v. Bertha

The sale of the building entitled Zerwitz to the same rights that Arnold had. Under the lease, Bertha owed Arnold (and now Zerwitz) a duty to maintain the property in good repair and not to sublease the property without Arnold's permission. Even if Bertha convinces the court that Arnold ratified the sublease to Carter by accepting rent from Carter, the sublease does not relieve Bertha of the duty to maintain the property in good repair and pay the rent. Only an assignment of the lease to Carter would relieve her of those responsibilities.

That the fire was caused by a negligent act with an illegal space heater is evidence that Bertha's failure to maintain the property in good repair occurred without a good excuse (i.e., it was a breach). Consequently, Zerwitz can demand damages in the amount of rent for the duration of the lease minus any rent received after Zerwitz rents the repaired building (Zerwitz has a duty to mitigate his damages by making a good faith attempt to rerent the building).

Zerwitz can also sue Bertha for breach of contract for failing to pay rent. Bertha's defense of impossibility will fail because the reason for the impossibility was Carter's negligence imputed to Bertha. Bertha may have a cause of action against Carter, but that does not relieve her of the duty to pay the rent.

Zerwitz v. Carter

Under the law of torts, Carter owed foreseeable plaintiffs like Zerwitz a duty of reasonable care. Therefore, Zerwitz can sue Carter for breach of that duty (negligence)—if he can find him. Zerwitz cannot sue Carter for breach of contract because Zerwitz has no privity of contract with Carter.

Zerwitz v. Arnold

Even if the court finds that Arnold ratified Bertha's sublease to Carter, Zerwitz still cannot sue Arnold for the equitable remedy of contribution because Arnold owes Zerwitz no duty—a landlord is not responsible for the negligent acts of his tenants.

Donna, et al. v. Zorro, et al.

On July 1, 1989, two weeks before they were married, Gary took his fiancee, Donna, to Zorro's Riding Stables to go horseback riding. Gary rented two horses from Zorro that Zorro personally selected. The horses were brought from the stables already saddled by Zorro's stable hand. Although Zorro made no inquiry as to prior riding experience, Donna had not been on a horse in recent years.

Zorro led Gary and Donna on their horses through a field and then out onto a small trail that Zorro had cleared on his property that ran parallel to the public highway. Shortly after reaching the trail, Gary's horse was startled when Bozo, a passenger in a passing car, threw away a beer can that struck Gary's horse. Gary's horse kicked, and in response Donna's horse reared. Although Donna grabbed the reins and saddlehorn, she and the saddle were thrown off. Donna suffered an acute lumbosacral sprain, which kept her off work for one week and also severely restricted her intimate relations with Gary on her honeymoon. Donna's doctor also told her that she will suffer from periodic back pain and have a "bad back" for some time.

Today, Gary and Donna have come to see you. They relate the above facts. They further inform you than an inspection of the saddle after the incident showed that one end of the girth had become untied and that the other end had broken, the leather strap showing evidence of dry rot. They also inform you that Zorro had failed to obtain the required license to operate a riding stable and that his stable had not been inspected in 1989, both as required by law, although his stables had been properly licensed and inspected in the past.

Analyze whether Gary, Donna, and Gary and Donna together have any causes of action, giving in your answer the parties to the cause of the action, the elements of the cause of action, the facts supporting such a cause of action, the nature of any potential recovery, and any anticipated defenses.

Discussion

If Donna's horse had not reared, the defective straps would not have caused any injury to Donna. Conversely, if the horse had reared but the straps were not defective, Donna would not have suffered an injury. Thus, two events—the defective straps and the thrown beer can—combined to cause Donna's injury. (The defective straps seem more important because anything that would have caused the horse to rear up would have resulted in Donna's injury.) With regard to the saddle, either one of the defective straps—the broken one or the untied one—could have caused Donna's injury.)

Gary and Donna v. Zorro Stables

Gary and Donna together have no cause of action for loss of consortium because under Maryland law, the right of consortium only exists in a marriage. Since Gary and Donna were not married, there was no damage to the enjoyment of their marriage.

Gary v. Zorro Stables

Zorro Stables owed Gary a contractual obligation to provide a safe horseback ride. Gary can sue Zorro Stables for breach of contract, but damages would only be the rental fee.

Having suffered no damages, Gary has no standing to sue Zorro Stables in torts. Also, he has no standing to sue for his pain and suffering at seeing his fiance injured. Even if he could prove that he suffered the required physical manifestations of pain and suffering, Maryland does not protect unmarried, unrelated couples from the emotional harm of seeing a loved one injured.

Gary v. Bozo

Under tort law, Bozo owed foreseeable plaintiffs a duty of reasonable care in disposing of empty beer cans. Gary would have a cause of action in torts for breaching that duty, except for the fact that Gary suffered no damages.

Donna v. Zorro Stables

Under tort law, Zorro Stables owed Donna a duty to use reasonable care to provide her a safe, properly equipped horse and a trail free of hazards. This duty is imposed by the fact that Donna was a fore-seeable plaintiff and by her status as a business invitee (someone welcomed on another's property for the purpose of benefitting the owner's business). The stable's duty to business invitees is to protect them from hazards that the stable could have discovered with rea-sonable care. The stable is also vicariously responsible for its em-ployees (Zorro and the stable hand) acting in the course of employ-ment.

The specific acts of negligence include Zorro's failure to inquire into Donna's riding experience and choose a horse that would not rear up (Donna will have to prove that Zorro knew or should have known that her horse would rear up); Zorro's failure to build the path away from a highway where passing cars or drivers might spook the horses; and the failure of the stable hand to secure one end of the girth and to inspect the other for dry rot.

Zorro's failure to obtain the required license to operate a riding stable would be negligence per se if Donna could show that renewal of the license would have included an inspection of Zorro's operating procedures. If so, the statute requiring a license was designed to protect people like Donna against the harm she suffered.

Donna may also have a torts claim against Zorro in strict liability if she can show that Zorro knew Donna's horse was likely to rear, making the horse unreasonably dangerous.

Donna v. Bozo

Like Gary, Donna can sue Bozo in torts for negligently tossing a beer can without looking at where it would land. Once she proves negligence, she should have no difficulty proving that the thrown beer can caused her horse to rear up resulting in her injuries.

Regardless of whom she sues, Donna will ask for monetary damages to cover her past and future medical expenses, lost wages, pain and suffering, and loss of future earning capacity.

Defenses

Zorro's Stable will raise the defense of assumption of risk since Donna got on the horse knowing that horses can rear up with little provocation, and that she had insufficient experience to handle that foreseeable event. Also, Donna was contributorily negligent for failing to inform Zorro of her novice status and for failing to ask about the horse's docility. Finally, while it might have been negligent to fail to check the saddle, the real cause of Donna's injury was the thrown beer can, an unforeseeable event that became an intervening superceding cause of Donna's injuries.

Bozo's defense is that what really caused Donna's injury were the broken saddle straps, an unforeseeable supervening event. His throwing of the beer was only a cause-in-fact of the injury, not the proximate cause of Donna's injury because no one could have predicted that the beer can would cause this injury.

Dorsey v. State

In 1989, the Dorsey Timber Corporation ("Dorsey") purchased "White Mud Farm," a 400-acre tract of largely wooded land located in the State of Westover for $500,000. Dorsey acquired the farm to remove its large stands of timber. Dorsey's decision to purchase the farm was based upon independent appraisals which valued the timber on the farm at $2,000,000. Under applicable law, no permits were required for Dorsey to conduct timbering operations on the property. Because of a slump in the construction industry, Dorsey deferred actual operations on the property until 1993.

In 1990, acting in response to public pressure, the legislature of the State of Westover conducted hearings on global atmospheric warming (i.e., the "greenhouse effect"). The evidence presented at the hearing showed 1) there was a deep division among respected scientific opinion as to whether the greenhouse effect presently existed and 2) if did exist, it was caused by a combination of atmospheric pollution and widespread destruction of forests.

As a result of the hearing, the legislature enacted the "Woodland Protection Act of 1990" (the "Act"). The Act defined woodlands and declared that they "constituted a vital and irreplaceable environmental asset" and that the destruction of woodlands located in Westover threatened the atmosphere.

The Act prohibited any activity in a woodland (as defined in the Act) which would result in the clearing of more than two (2) acres of trees. The Act contained two exemptions: 1) it permitted residential development of any woodland less than 15 acres in size and 2) it allowed timbering in any woodland if "the woodland area subject to timbering is part of a farm which is owned by persons who derive at least 75% of their annual income from farming activities." The Act became effective on December 31, 1990. The Act was adopted in accordance with all procedural requirements of the State of Westover.

Seventy per cent (70%) of White Mud Farm is woodland as defined in the Act. Dorsey estimates that, as a result of the Act, and taking the purchase price into consideration, it will not be profitable to carry on any timbering operations on the farm. Dorsey can prove that, as a result of the Act, the value of the farm has fallen to $250,000. Dorsey has filed suit to challenge the validity of the Act or, alternatively, to obtain compensation for the loss in value of its investment. Assume that you are Dorsey's lawyer. What arguments would you advance to support Dorsey's position? What is the probable outcome?

Discussion

Under the Fifth Amendment of the Constitution, the government owes citizens a duty not to deprive them of their property without due process, or take their property for a public purpose without just compensation. Dorsey should argue that by directly affecting 70% of his property and reducing its value from more than $2,000,000 to only $250,000, the statute deprived him of over $1,750,000 in property. The state did this without due process (a hearing) thereby breaching its duty of due process, and it took his property for the public good without fair compensation—both a clear breach of its duty under the Fifth Amendment. The state will defend with the argument that his property was not physically taken, only limited in what could be done to it. Moreover, Dorsey has lost only $250,000, not the $1,750,000 he claims.

Under the Fourteenth Amendment, the government owes its citizens a duty to enact legislation that has some rational expectation of fulfilling a legitimate state interest. Dorsey should argue that there is no rational reason to expect the statute to accomplish the state's admittedly legitimate interest in reducing the greenhouse effect. The facts reflect a deep division among scientists whether there is a greenhouse problem, and whether deforestation is a significant cause. This argument will likely fail as the courts generally defer to the legislature on areas requiring expert testimony.

Under the Equal Protection clause of the Fourteenth Amendment, the government owes its citizens a duty to treat them equally, unless the government has some good reason for favoring one group over another. In this case, the statute allows farmers and residential developers to deforest their property. However, since the discrimination is not based on race, religion, or country of origin, the state need only show some rational reason for its decision to discriminate against those not engaged in farming or residential development. In order to survive an Equal Protection challenge, the state need only claim that it wants to encourage farming or real estate development. Dorsey is likely to lose on an Equal Protection challange.

Estate of John

John, a widower, was the owner of a 100-acre farm in Calvert County, Maryland. John lived there with his unmarried daughter, Jane. John's only other child, Hanna, lived in Baltimore. John executed a valid deed dated and acknowledged on January 2, 1980, conveying the entire farm to Jane. John gave the deed to his faithful friend and minister the Reverend Jim with instructions "to hold it until my death and then give it to Jane."

Ten years later, on his death bed, John executed a valid will devising $10,000 to his daughter Jane and all of the remainder of his estate including his real estate to his daughter Hanna. John died on January 15, 1990, and Jane, who knew of his will and the deed, promptly went to the Reverend Jim and demanded the deed. The Reverend Jim, not knowing the contents of the will, turned the deed over to Jane, who promptly recorded it among the Calvert County Land Records.

Hanna is claiming the farm belongs to her, and Jane comes to you for clarification of her rights.

Discussion

This case does not involve duties, but rather—as is common in real property law—the nature of the property interest, i.e., the triggering event that *defines* the duties.

If Jane had had possession of the deed before her father's death, she could obviously claim ownership to the farm. With the deed in Reverend Jim's possession, Jane could still claim that she had "constructive" possession of the deed because no one else but she had rights to the deed. The reason for this is that when her father gave the deed to Reverend Jim, he relinquished control of the deed, including his right to revoke it.

Further discovery will be necessary to determine whether John gave the Reverend the deed with the intent of permanently placing it beyond his legal reach. From the facts alone, it does not appear that John surrendered legal control of the deed.

If the court finds that Jane could not claim title to the farm until she obtained the deed after her father's death, her recording of the deed had no effect because in Maryland it would only protect Jane against subsequent purchasers. Hanna was an heir, not a purchaser who needed to be on notice of a prior deed. In other jurisdictions, Jane's recording of the deed might prevail.

Jack & Jill v. Lucky Lanes, et al.

Jack and Jill Waters were members of a weekly bowling league. Every Friday night for the past year, they have bowled tenpins at Lucky Lanes in Frederick, Maryland.

During one Friday evening session, Jack, who weighs some 250 lbs., went to the refreshment area. After purchasing a soda, Jack sat in one of the molded fiberglass chairs that were placed around the tables. Several friends sat with him in the other chairs. While Jack consumed his soda, the chair in which he was sitting collapsed, and he fell to the floor and sustained injury to his lower back and knees.

Following the incident, Lucky Lanes management prepared an accident report and noted that the bolts holding the molded fiberglass seat to the steel leg unit had broken, thereby allowing the legs to become detached from the seat. The chair was inadvertently disposed of by Lucky Lanes.

Lucky Lanes purchased all of its furniture for the alleys from King Supply Company. The chairs in the refreshment area were replaced when visibly worn. Periodically, additional chairs were purchased for the refreshment area. Chairs had been purchased by Lucky through King in 1985, 1987, and 1989. The original order for chairs was placed in 1982, when the alleys were renovated and all-new furniture was purchased.

King Supply purchases the chairs directly from the manufacturer Seats-a-Plenty. The chairs purchased by King for the refreshment area are always the same model, Number A–1. Shipments from Seats-a-Plenty are made by rail delivery. The fiberglass seats and steel-legged units are shipped together but unassembled. King must secure the steel legs to the seats with screws and washers provided by Seats-a-Plenty.

Discussion

Jack v. Lucky Lanes

As the owner of a business being patronized by Jack, a business invitee, Lucky Lanes owed a duty to Jack under tort law to use reasonable care to ensure the safety of its customers. This means inspecting the property to discover hazards that its customers would not reasonably discover themselves.

In this case, Lucky Lanes owed Jack a duty to inspect its chairs for defects. To prove that Lucky breached its duty, Jack will have to prove that Lucky Lanes failed to inspect the chairs or, if it did, it failed to see the defective bolts which any reasonable inspection would have uncovered.

Jack v. King Supply

Under products liability law (torts), King Supply owed potential users of the products it assembled a duty of reasonable care to ensure their safety when using those products. This means inspecting and testing the product for reasonably apparent defects. King cannot assert the "sealed container" defense because King opened the containers and assembled the chairs shipped to it by Seat-a-Plenty. (Under the sealed container defense, the distributor is under no duty to open the container to inspect and test the product unless the container is damaged enough to put the distributor on notice of a defective product inside.)

To prove King breached its duty, Jack must prove that the bolts broke because King 1) improperly assembled the chair, 2) failed to inspect the chair for broken bolts, or 3) failed to test the chair to ensure that repeated use would not cause the bolts to break.

Jack can also sue King Supply under strict liability, because in Maryland an assembler of an unreasonably dangerous product is as liable as the manufacturer. The defect making the product unreasonably dangerous can be a flaw in the design of the product, a flaw in the manufacture of the product, or a failure to warn of risks in using the product.

Jack also has a claim under breach of warranty even though he did not buy the seat, because Maryland has extended standing to sue under breach of warranty to potential users of the product. King may have given Lucky Lanes an express warranty about the chairs, but if it didn't, it still owed Lucky Lanes a duty to provide a safe product under the implied warranty of merchantability and warranty of fitness for a particular purpose. Jack should have no trouble proving the seat was unsafe, and therefore that King breached its duty under warranty law.

Jack v. Seats-a-Plenty

Jack can assert a products liability claim against Seats-a-Plenty, claiming that the manufacturer of a product owes potential users a duty to reasonably design, manufacture, test, and inspect its product, and to warn of any hazards in using the product.

Jack can assert a claim of strict liability against Seats-a-Plenty as the manufacturer of the seat. (If it turns out the bolt was made by a manufacturer "upstream," Seats-a-Plenty would still be held in strict liability as an assembler.)

Jack v. Bolt Manufacturer

Jack can sue the bolt manufacturer for negligence and strict liability. To prove any of his negligence claims, however, Jack must establish the exact reason the bolts broke. Unfortunately, the chair was "inadvertently disposed of by Lucky Lanes," making it impossible for Jack to determine why the bolts broke. Therefore, Jack must use res ipsa loquitur to prove his claim: a chair does not break in the absence of negligence; the defendant had exclusive control of the chair; and nothing Jack did contributed to the broken chair. This will force the defendant to come forward with evidence in its control that it was not negligent. The defendants will defend with the fact that they did not have exclusive control of the chairs because the public also had access to them.

Against Jack's negligence claims, the defendants can raise the following defense of contributory negligence: Jack, knowing he was heavy, "plopped" onto the chair when he sat down. This defense will likely fail because Jack had no reasonable expectation the chair would collapse. Against Jack's strict liability claim, the defendant cannot raise a defense of contributory negligence.

Jack will sue for his medical expenses, any lost wages, lost future earnings, and pain and suffering. As a married couple, Jack and Jill can claim loss of consortium.

Tina v. Lark

Lark, Inc. owns and manages a garden apartment building in Baltimore County. Tina signed a one-year lease for an apartment on the first floor, beginning January 1, 1991. The relevant terms of Tina's form lease, and those of all other tenants, prohibited the keeping of pets and occupancy by more than two persons, unless the landlord gave permission. The form lease also required the tenant "to deposit all trash in the dumpster provided by Landlord."

In March 1991, Jake and his two male roommates signed a form lease for the apartment next to Tina's. Lark, Inc. gave express permission to allow occupancy by three adults and to allow Jake to keep his bulldog in the apartment.

Since March 1991, Tina has had numerous problems with her three neighbors. Tina has to fend off Jake's constant suggestions that she join him and his roommates for explicit sexual activity; Jake's roommates often leave beer cans and trash in the common hallway; and

Jake's bulldog growls menacingly every time it sees Tina, causing her to become genuinely terrified.

Stan, a newly admitted attorney who lives in the same building as Tina, has witnessed these events and wants to help her. Stan told Tina to write a letter to Lark, Inc. complaining about Jake and his room-mates. On April 15, 1991, Tina wrote a detailed letter to the apartment manager, explaining the problems and asking Lark, Inc. to "do whatever is necessary to correct the situation." After investigating Tina's com-plaints, the manager advised Jake and his roommates to keep the hallways free of trash, and they complied with the landlord's directive. However, Tina's problems with Jake's offensive comments and his bulldog continued.

For this reason, Tina moved out of Lark's apartment building on May 31, 1991. She spent several nights in a motel before finding a comparable apartment, which costs $20 more per month than the one she had leased from Lark, Inc.

Tina has just been served with a District Court complaint by Lark, Inc., claiming rent since June 1, 1991. Tina asks Stan to explain in detail her legal rights and obligations and to represent her in the action filed by Lark, Inc.. What should Stan tell Tina?

Discussion

First, Stan should inform Tina that he cannot represent her because he may be called as a witness, and as her lawyer he will not be permitted to testify (because there would be too much bias in his testimony).

Having clarified that he cannot be her attorney, Stan can then inform Tina that under contract law, she owes Lark a duty to pay rent as stated in the lease—unless she has a good excuse for not paying rent. Such an excuse might be found in real property law: every lease has an implied covenant of quiet enjoyment imposing a duty on the land-lord not to interfere with a tenant's use and enjoyment of his apart-ment. The landlord's failure to perform this duty without an excuse— an excuse being lack of notice about the problem, impossibility of

124 / Learning Law

correcting the problem, or insufficient time to correct the problem—
constitutes a breach, allowing the tenant to treat the lease as terminated and move out without paying further rent.

Since Lark did correct the garbage problem, Tina will have to prove
that her use and enjoyment of the apartment were interfered with by
Jake's offensive remarks and by the dog's growling. The former is
believable, but she will have a difficult time proving that a dog which
only growled as she entered and exited her apartment interfered
significantly with her use and enjoyment of the apartment. If Tina *can*
show significant interference, she will still have to prove that, included
in Lark's duty not to interfere with her enjoyment of the apartment,
was the duty to control Jake's dog and Jake's offensive remarks. Tina
will then have to prove that Lark had the authority to control Jake's
dog and Jake's offensive remarks. Further discovery may uncover that
the dog was kept in a common area under the landlord's control, but
proving Lark had authority to control Jake's speech will be difficult.

As landlord, Lark also owed Tina a duty under real property law
not to constructively evict her—interfere with her use and enjoyment
to such an extent that she could not reasonably stay there. Breach of
this duty would allow Tina to sue for the expenses of finding a new
apartment, moving, and any increase in rent for the duration of the
lease. Failure to prove this claim, however, will subject Tina (under
breach of contract) to liability for the rent until the apartment is re-
rented, which Lark has a duty to do as part of his common law duty
to mitigate damages.

Epson v. Sanyo

On June 1, 1985, Epson became an employee of Sanyo, which sold
and serviced all types of business and office machines. Two years later,
Sanyo asked Epson, along with other salesmen, to sign an agreement
not to compete with Sanyo should they ever leave the company. Epson
declined to sign the agreement. Thereafter Epson was informed by
Sanyo that he would be discharged if he did not agree to sign the
agreement. Because Epson had pressing financial obligations, he

knuckled under and signed the agreement providing that if he left Sanyo's employment he would not compete with Sanyo in the selling of merchandise or wares of any kind sold by Sanyo for three years within a 100-mile radius of the City of Baltimore, Maryland.

During his employment Epson was compensated on a commission basis. However, in January 1991 he was unsuccessful in collecting all of his year-end commissions and decided at that time to leave Sanyo and set up his own business in downtown Baltimore servicing business equipment. Epson informed Sanyo of his decision to leave May 1, 1991 and departed amicably on June 1, 1991. Between May 1 and June 1, Sanyo gave Epson permission to bid on a service contract with a former customer which Sanyo did not intend to pursue and which Epson successfully negotiated in Baltimore.

On July 15, 1991, Sanyo, relying on the agreement signed by Epson in 1987, demanded that Epson stop further competition with Sanyo, which Epson refused to do. Epson has now come to see you and asks you whether Sanyo can prevent Epson from engaging in his business. How would you analyze 1) Sanyo's arguments for enforcement of the agreement and 2) Epson's arguments to defeat the enforcement of the agreement?

Discussion

Sanyo is asserting that under contract law Epson owes it a duty to abide by the terms of the non-competition clause of his contract. Epson's defense is that under the common law of employment contracts, a non-competition clause is only enforceable against an employee if 1) the non-competition clause is justified to protect business trade secrets, customer lists, goodwill, etc.; 2) the clause is supported by adequate consideration; 3) the restrictive area and duration of non-competition to protect the employer's business are not too extreme; 4) the non-competition clause does not prevent the employee from obtaining employment in his field; and 5) the clause does not adversely affect the public interest.

Sanyo's position is that continued employment was adequate consideration for Epson. Whether three years and a 100-mile radius is unduly restrictive will require further discovery of Sanyo's goodwill and its competition in the region. From the facts, it appears that the clause imposes a hardship on Epson, but does not prevent him from learning how to repair other types of machines and selling service contracts on them.

Epson's defenses are, first, that the clause never referred to the sale of service contracts, only to the sale of merchandise and wares. Wares should not include services. Also, the clause is unenforceable because it was extracted under duress. Whether the threat of being fired forced Epson to sign is doubtful because Epson could have quit and worked elsewhere. Epson will argue that three years and a 100-mile radius is too extreme; Sanyo cannot possibly service that large an area in a competitive manner. Epson can also claim that Sanyo already breached the contract by failing to pay all of his commissions, and therefore, he no longer owes Sanyo a duty to perform the terms of the contract. Finally, Epson will argue that Sanyo waived its right to enforce the non-competition clause when it allowed Epson to bid on a service contract with one of Sanyo's former customers. Using estoppel theory, Epson relied to his detriment (e.g., renting a repair shop) on Sanyo's permission to bid on one of Sanyo's customers.

Able v. Baker

Able was selling his real estate known as "Moon Glow" for $1.5 million. This real property contained between six and seven acres of land and was improved by a 50-year-old, six-bedroom house.

Able showed the property to Baker. Baker was particularly interested in the property boundaries as he had plans to sell timber from some areas of the property. In the course of their on-site inspection, Able mistakenly described the southern boundary of the property as 2500 feet by referring to the wrong oak tree along the southern edge of the property. The actual length of the southern boundary was 1900 feet.

After walking the property with Able, Baker verbally offered $1.2 million; Able accepted. Baker then had his attorney prepare the agreement of sale. The agreement of sale contained a metes and bounds description and referenced a recorded plat of survey of the property, both of which gave the correct description. Able and Baker signed the agreement of sale. Settlement took place on June 20, 1990. The deed was properly recorded.

Shortly after taking possession of "Moon Glow" in July 1990, Baker was mowing the grass along what he believed to be the southern boundary of his property. His neighbor to the south, Charlie, came over to him and, in good spirits, thanked him for mowing his (Charlie's) property. Baker was surprised.

Nothing further happened regarding the boundary until March 1991. At that time, Baker ordered and a received a survey of "Moon Glow" which had been done at Baker's request for the construction of tennis courts on the property. This survey described the southern boundary as 1900 feet, not 2500 feet. Baker called Able about this, but Able refused to do anything.

Baker put in the tennis courts on his property in April at a cost of $11,000. Baker then sued Able on June 19, 1991, for rescission of the contract.

Discussion

Baker has a duty under the terms of the contract to pay Able $1.2 million for Moon Glow—unless he can find an excuse to rescind the contract. Baker is relying on a mutual mistake stemming from Able's mistaken oral description of the southern boundary of the property. While the property line was a fundamental aspect of the contract (Baker planned to sell the timber on the property), there is doubt about whether, in fact, a mutual mistake was made about the boundary line. Baker's attorney prepared the deed with the correct land measurements, and this knowledge is imputed to Baker. Also, when Baker signed the deed he presumably read the deed and agreed to the land's measurements. Baker cannot now change the deed because of Able's oral description; in the absence of fraud, oral statements prior to a contract cannot change an unambiguous contract (parol evidence rule).

Baker's failure to notify Able of the mistake for nine months can be construed as a ratification of the mistake. Even stronger evidence that Baker ratified the deed is his building of a tennis court on the property.

Baker can also try basing his claim in equity—on a quantum meruit theory of unjust enrichment. Having received less than he bargained for, Baker paid more than she should have. This will be difficult to prove since Baker actually paid $300,000 less than Able initially asked.

Homer v. Jethro

Homer owned a building situated on Route 40 near Ellicott City. Jethro, a friend of Homer, and an antique collector of some reputation, entered into a written agreement with Homer to open an antique shop in Homer's building. The contract provided that Homer would supply the building, all utilities and $40,000 cash for the purchase of antiques. Jethro was to supply $10,000 for the purchase of antiques. Jethro's investment in the venture was to be repaid as such time as the business terminated, or in 10 years from the date of the contract, whichever first occurred. Jethro was to manage the shop, make the purchases and establish the price of the merchandise. He was to be compensated at the rate of $200 per week plus 7% of gross receipts. It was further agreed that 50% of the net profits would be used to purchase additional merchandise with the balance to be paid to Homer. The enterprise did business as "Treasure Trove Antique Emporium."

After three years of operations, the business became embroiled in litigation with Trash for Cash, Inc., its principal supplier of antiques. The suit involved a disputed debt claimed by Trash for Cash of $8000 for merchandise purchased by Jethro, and invoiced to Treasure Trove Antique Emporium. Defendants in the case are Treasure Trove Antique Emporium and Homer and Jethro as partners.

Can Trash for Cash recover against Jethro? If so, can Jethro recover from Homer?

Discussion

Trash for Cash can recover against Jethro if it can prove under the common (or statutory) law of partnerships that Jethro was a partner in the Treasure Trove Antique Emporium, because partners are jointly and severally liable for all debts of the partnership. The best test of a partnership is whether the profits were divided among the parties. This does not mean using the profits to pay back one party's investment in the company or to pay one party's salary, but rather a real sharing of the profits (the sharing does not have to be equal). A convincing test for sharing of profits would be if Jethro's salary were suspended during periods of no profit. Since that is not the case here, the intent of the partners was probably not to form a partnership. As for Jethro's initial $10,000 "investment," it had to be repaid, indicating that it was a loan not an investment.

Jethro could still be considered Homer's partner under equity law if Jethro and Homer expressly or implicitly said or did something to make Trash believe that Jethro was a partner, and in reliance on that belief, Trash extended credit to the Treasure Trove. In this case, the name Treasure Trove Antique Emporium did not contain Jethro's name, but the stationery and the company checks should be examined for Jethro's name. Also, how Jethro signed the checks needs to be discovered.

Trash can also recover against Jethro under the common (or statutory) law of agency if it can prove that as Homer's agent, Jethro acted beyond his authority. This seems unlikely because Jethro was in charge of buying antiques from Trash.

John v. Sheila

John, an advertising broker, had been discussing with Sheila, a printer, the production of some advertising brochures for one of John's clients, Evertrue Insurance Agency. On June 5, John wrote Sheila the following letter:

Dear Sheila:

This will confirm my order for printing services. You will print 100,000 Evertrue brochures on paper supplied by us per sample previously submitted. Price to be 5 cents a brochure. Delivery will be in lots of 20,000 each on successive Fridays beginning June 17th. Time is of the essence. Payment upon receipt.

John

Sheila did not reply to the letter until after she had delivered the first 20,000 brochures on June 17. At that time, she told John's secretary to remind him that in their earlier discussions, she had told John that the timing of delivery was uncertain because of the workload of her shop. John's secretary paid for the June 17 delivery with one of John's checks and later that day, told John of her conversation with Sheila.

On June 20 Sheila wrote John the following letter.

Dear John:

I cannot make the delivery schedule you propose unless I put on extra help, and the price will be 10 cents per brochure.

Sheila

John received the letter on June 21, but did not reply. On June 24, Sheila delivered the second 20,000 brochures to John and presented an invoice for $2,000. John refused to pay the invoice insisting he had not agreed to pay anymore than five cents a brochure, and that he was cancelling the order.

A) The same day Sheila calls you, her attorney, for advice. In your discussion with Sheila, cover her legal position. What action can she take and what is your opinion as to the chances of her success?

B) Larry is John's attorney and spends a great deal of time at John's office negotiating on John's behalf some of his more complicated brokerage deals, and dealing with controversies that develop. He has become quite familiar with all aspects of the advertising brokerage business. Sheila had never dealt directly with Larry, but John had told her of Larry's activities on his behalf and had stated on several occasions that Larry was his "right-hand man and knew as much about the advertising brokerage business as anyone."

Assuming the same factual situation as in Part A and as above, would your advice to Sheila be different if Sheila were met at the time of the first delivery, not by John's secretary, but by Larry who told her,

"John probably won't remember your conversation, but the price looks good to me, so go ahead"?

Discussion

A) Sheila should prepare to use two branches of the law to impose a duty of performance on John—the UCC and the law of contracts. While at first blush their contract appears to be for goods (UCC)—brochures—in fact, John was ordering "printing *services*" using paper supplied by him (contract law).

Under the UCC, there appears to be a valid offer in the letter sent to Sheila and signed by John describing the item ordered, the quantity, and the price. Between merchants like Sheila and John, the offeree can accept by delivering the goods, so Sheila's acceptance of the check and delivery of the goods clearly complete the elements for a valid contract. Sheila is thus bound to the terms in John's letter. Any previous discussions with John justifying delivery of the goods at a later time at a higher price would be barred by the parol evidence rule since such discussions would directly contradict the terms of the contract ("Price to be 5 cents a brochure . . . time is of the essence").

The only way for Sheila to increase the five-cent fee would be to convince the court that her letter constituted an offer to modify the contract, an offer that was accepted by John's silence as allowed under the UCC. John may be able to defend as follows: if Sheila could not deliver the goods as stated in his letter, she should not have accepted his terms. Therefore, her attempt to change the terms in midstream without a change in circumstances was an act of bad faith not requiring an answer from him. The court is likely find that under the UCC, John had a duty to answer Sheila's letter. Whether three days (June 20 to June 23) was enough time for John to reply to Sheila's letter will be a jury question.

If the court finds that this was a service contract governed by contract law, there would still be a valid contract. John's offer described the item, the quantity, the price, and the delivery terms, and Sheila's delivery constituted acceptance by partial performance. However, Sheila's offer to modify the contract contained no new consideration and was never accepted by John. Therefore, her letter had no effect on her original obligation to supply the brochures for five cents apiece. Whether the court will allow John to cancel the contract without first waiting to see if Sheila would fail to deliver any more brochures will depend on whether a reasonable person would have believed that Sheila was not going deliver the rest of the brochures without an increase in price (anticipatory breach).

If Sheila convinces the court that the UCC governs, she will likely prevail, in which case she should ask the court for specific performance and monetary damages.

B) Sheila can hold John to Larry's acceptance of her increase in price if she can prove under the common (or statutory) law of agency that Larry was John's agent acting within the scope of his responsibility. There are four ways to prove that an agent had the authority to contract. The principal may have *expressly* granted the authority, either orally or by written agreement. The principal may have *implied* the authority through prior dealings with the agent. The principal may have expressly told or, through acts, implied to the third party that he had granted the agent *apparent* authority to contract. Finally, the principal may have *ratified* the agent's actions by accepting the benefits of the contract, even though the agent acted without authority.

By telling Sheila "of Larry's (past) activities on his behalf... and ... that Larry was his right-hand man," John gave Sheila the reasonable impression that Larry had apparent authority to act on John's behalf. Whether this was a reasonable inference on Sheila's part is a jury question.